ISLAM AND GOD-CENTRICITY: PLURALITY AND MUTABILITY OF RELIGION

by

Shaykh Arif Abdul Hussain

Printed in the United Kingdom.

ISBN 978-1-9998621-7-6

Published by:
Sajjadiyya Press
60 Weoley Park Road
Selly Oak
Birmingham, B29 6RB

Author: Shaykh Arif Abdul Hussain

CONTENTS

ACKNOWLEDGEMENTS

The following lectures were delivered at the Organisation of Islamic Learning (Toronto, Canada) on the first ten nights of Muharram 1440 (September 2018). The author wishes to express his sincere gratitude to the community and its committee members for graciously hosting the lectures. He also wishes to thank Ms Samar Mashhadi for transcribing the lectures and the initial edit of this book, Mr Riaz Walji for subsequent rearrangements and final edits, and Shaykh Mahmood Dhalla for the proof reading and his invaluable and critical feedback.

FOREWORD:

In the name of God, the All-Beneficent, the All-Merciful
All praise belongs to God.
May benedictions and peace be upon Muhammad,
His apostle and the best of His creation,
And upon the Pure Ones of his family,
And upon the Noble Souls who supported his mission.

THIS BOOK IS THE FOURTH VOLUME in the *Islam and God-Centricity* series. It is comprised of the edited transcripts of the lectures delivered by Shaykh Arif Abdul Hussain in Muharram 1440 (September 2018). The main themes of the book are religious pluralism, the mutability of religion, and salvation. The lectures in this book are a continuation of the previous volumes' lectures, and so they too presume that the purpose of religion is to facilitate human growth and evolution, and thereby to establish the *khilāfa* of Allah upon this earth. They introduce the reader to the notions of 'form' and 'essence' and how they are existential, that is, their purpose is only 'growth' to Allah. The basic thesis of this book is that the problems facing Muslims today, such as religious exclusivism, sectarianism, and accusations of the archaic-ness of Muslim societal regulations, are due to Muslims mistaking the 'forms' of religion for the 'essence' of religion. By distinguishing between the two, and understanding the specific and general purposes and characteristics of each, Muslims are able to separate the 'forms' from the 'essence' of religion; they can then reformulate befitting 'forms' in light of the 'essence' of religion for newer contexts. The result is our acceptance of religious and legal pluralism as existential facts, and the understanding that the notions of salvific exclusivism and the immutability of the regulations of the Quran and hadith literature are aberrations in the history of Muslim thought.

The lecture titles/themes are as follows:

Lecture 1: the Essence and Form of Religion
Lecture 2: Diversity of Forms
Lecture 3: Religious Exclusivism
Lecture 4: Spiritual Morality and No-Finality of Sharias
Lecture 5: the Mutability of the Quranic Regulations
Lecture 6: the Milla of Ibrahim, and Dīn
Lecture 7: Quran as a Contextual Expression of the Book
Lecture 8: the Finality of the Sharia
Lecture 9: the Plurality and Relativity of Collectivities
Lecture 10: Salvation

The following terms or expressions occur frequently throughout the book and are used to refer to meanings that may be different to their ordinary usage:

- The word 'collectivity' (pl. 'collectivities') is a general word referring to every type of human grouping, irrespective of whether they are natural and/or based on ideology, philosophy, or otherwise. It refers to the family, tribe, community, society, nation, and global human community. It can be used to refer to any one, some, or all of them.

- The phrase 'existential aptitudes' (or just 'aptitudes') refers to the psychological, cognitive, and moral aptitudes of the human individual and collectivity. They are subject to change and growth during the lifetime of both the individual and collectivity. They differ between individuals of the same collectivity and also between different collectivities.

- The expressions 'the existential property of growth' and 'evolutionary motion' refer to the fact that manifested existence is in a state of perpetual change and growth.

Hence, 'growth' is a property of existence, or an 'existential property'. Existence is continually actualising its outer and inner potential and is always in a state of 'growth' outwardly and inwardly. The individual human being, the collectivity of human beings, and human beings as one historical continuum, are subject to rational, moral, and spiritual growth.

- The expression 'human nobility' denotes that nobility is the essence of humankind. It refers to the inherent sense of compassion, decency, and godliness within each individual. As such, 'human nobility' is in a constant state of refinement. Human reason and all other faculties of the soul operate according to the degree of growth of 'human nobility'.

- The phrase 'the principle of justice' refers to the propensity in human beings to understand what is 'just' in any given time and place; however, such understanding is always contingent upon the degree of growth of 'human nobility' of the collectivity of that time and place. Thus, what is deemed to be 'just' by the collectivity of a particular time and place may not be deemed as such by the collectivity of another time and place, due to the increased 'growth' in the 'human nobility' of the latter collectivity.

- The word '*ḥanīf*' is frequently used in the Quran to refer to Prophet Ibrahim. It is usually translated as 'an upright man', however this translation does not capture the true significance of the word, which is 'a man who distinguishes the truth from the false, the good from the bad, and the beautiful from the ugly, and hence is established in the Truth, the Good, and the Beautiful'. As such, no English word is able to convey this sense, and so the English transliteration '*ḥanīf*' will be used in this book to signify 'a man of the Truth, the Good, and the Beautiful'.

- The word 'sharia' means a body of devotional and societal regulations. The non-italicised singular word 'Sharia' with uppercase 'S' refers to the body of regulations of the religion of Prophet Muhammad. The italicised singular word *sharia* with lowercase 's' refers to the body of regulations of the religion of a prophet other than Prophet Muhammad, and the plural word *sharias* refers to several or all the different bodies of regulations of the prophets.

- The Quran has used the word 'islām' with two different meanings: 'surrendering to God', and as a formal designation for the organised religion of Prophet Muhammad. This will be discussed in detail in the book. However, it should be noted that from the middle of Lecture 3 onwards, the italicised word *islām* with lowercase 'i' refers to 'surrendering to the will of God', and the non-italicised word 'Islam' with uppercase 'I' refers to the organised formalised religion of the blessed Prophet. Accordingly, the italicised word *muslim* with lowercase 'm' refers to a practitioner of *islām* (that is, 'one surrendering to the will of God'), and the non-italicised word 'Muslim' with uppercase 'M' refers to an adherent of formal Islam.

The lectures in this book cover the following topics: religious pluralism and exclusivism; legal pluralism and the mutability of the Sharia; the notion of 'spiritual morality'; the nature of the Quran and our assumptions regarding it; the existential principle of 'no-finality'; and the plurality and relativity of collectivities.

Lecture One
The Essence and Form
of Religion

We are grateful to Allah for allowing us this opportunity to have these discussions in the name of our most beloved Imam Husayn. His demeanour and actions on the Day of Ashura, and in the months leading up to it, reveal a greater sense of purpose. They assure us of the meaningfulness of human existence and the necessity to avail the opportunity of life. This means we need to understand what we are and where we are headed so that we can lead a full and substantive life.

These lectures are a continuation of talks I have delivered over the past three years on 'Islam and God-centricity'. In this series, we will be delving into the same themes but from the 'form-essence' perspective of the existential framework.

Intuitively – by which I mean, *from the depths of our human condition* – we know that we are all one people, one human family, just as we know intuitively that God must be a beautiful God even before He informs us of His Own Self. We know deep within ourselves that we cannot surrender to a God who is less than absolutely Perfect: His charitable nature should know no limits, His knowledge no ignorance, and He must be mercy in its entirety. He is the Parent of all parents, the Love of all love, and the

Light of all light. None is like Him, and none is as immediate as He is, for He is closer to us than our jugular veins. He is always by our side, for He is our constant Companion. He accepts us for who and what we are, encourages us when we are defeated, and lifts us when we fall. He responds to us when we call Him. Recall Imam Husayn's supplication during his final breaths: 'O the One who is most proximate! O the One Who responds the moment I call unto Him!'

Thus, we know intuitively that our God is a most splendid God, and that He cannot be prejudicial. We know our God accepts every genuine gesture offered to Him, and that He has our best interest at heart; He wishes for all of us to succeed. We know He is needless and that we are in a state of need, and beyond that He is our only need. We also know that He will not oblige us, rather He takes pleasure in fulfilling our needs, and that He rejoices in whatever He has made. We call Him by the name 'God' or 'Allah'. For Him all are equal. He responds to all equally irrespective of whether we call Him with the eloquence of Imam Ali or broken words. No language prevails over another language as far as He is concerned, and no voice is preferred by Him over another. When the knowledge of all this is within us, and we know that He is our goal and direction, then why are we – the people of faith – not one human family in His name? Why do we make claims of *exclusivity* and superiority in His name?

To understand how this happens, let us consider the outset of our human journey. When we observe little children, their state of innocence is such that it displays their godliness. They do not understand gender distinction or discrimination based on colour and religion; they do not recognise any of these things. Their innocence brings them together: A boy and girl sit together, as does the black child and white child, and the rich child and poor child. They do not comprehend any distinction. In their innocence, they are one family.

Soon after setting off on their lives' journeys, their innocence is gradually eroded, and their minds tainted. They are taught that the colours and genders of their bodies are significant, the religion of their birth is the one true religion, and their particular familial, communal, and national statuses are better than all others. Before they know it, they feel they are the bodies in which they have taken birth, that is, they believe they are the genders of their bodies and the transient colours of their skins. Soon after that, they believe the religion of their parents is the only true religion and their familial, communal, and national identities are the best. At this point, the mind becomes plagued with superiority claims of 'I am better than him' and 'I am better than you'. The justifications for such superiority claims are supplied by religions, cultures, races, and communities. This marks the beginning of the exploitation of the 'other'. Thereafter, the differences between 'us' and 'them' are continually reinforced by all manner of familial, communal, cultural, and societal norms and attitudes.

As these young people begin to grow, they see the similarities and differences afresh. They begin to question: 'Does not red blood flow beneath the skin in all of us? Is the redness of that substance not equally shared by all? Do we not all pain in the same way? Do we not all feel hunger in the same way? Are we not all the same beyond the differences?' After this, there is the stage of critically analysing things; they perceive the differences that set them apart as arbitrary differences of 'the body' and 'the bodily', that is, they are seen to be merely 'formal' differences (or differences in forms) and not 'essential' differences. They realise that beyond the differences, there is unity in human values, that is, the noble human goals and aspirations. This is the journey of every individual: We are born in the cradle of innocence and godliness, after which the attitude of difference, division, and separation prevails. Finally, human reason becomes activated cutting through these surface 'formal' differences and divisions so that the deeper 'essential' commonalties are seen.

Observe the history of the human race: We have killed, butchered and massacred ourselves in the name of cultures, religions, nation-states, and political ideologies. Despite all of this, we are approaching that godly human pedestal where we understand, acknowledge, and proclaim that it is our humanity that makes us human, and not the colours of our faces, genders, locations, cultures, religions, nation-states, or political ideologies. Our 'essential' feature is that we are all thinking, feeling beings. Everything else is arbitrary. At the third stage of our journey, we cut through the false, superficial, and arbitrary differences with human reason and arrive at those salient truths.

Today, the notion of inalienable human rights is accepted universally as being patently true. It is obvious that no one should go to bed starving, every person should have autonomy in principle, and all of us have the right to life and education. This is understood as what is owed to every human being by virtue of being a human being; hence, discriminating between humans on the basis of any difference is not possible with regard to these inalienable rights. The discourse on human rights and its codification by international bodies and institutions is indicative of the fruition of human reason and rational thought. The same process of 'continual progression' occurs in religious communities.

Every faith that is monotheistic 'in essence' – such as the Abrahamic faiths, Hinduism, and Sikhism – claims that their God is the only One True God. This is like each of us saying, 'My God is the only One True God. Even though you are calling the same God, you have not understood Him properly.' Here I am admitting that my God is your God, and you also admit that your God is my God. Now if your God is my God and my God is your God, then He is one and the same God. Does that not make us the same? Can He communicate something to you which is different to what He has communicated to me 'in essence'? If we accept that we all believe and worship the same God, then we will have to accept that His communications have been multiple and that the 'essence' of each of them must be one and the same.

What does He want from us? My God is a kind God. He has not brought me into this world to waste me. Your God does not want to waste anybody either, or are we claiming that my God does not want to waste me, but He is more than happy to waste you? Then in that case I will put a big question mark over my God's benevolence. I can never admit that my God wants to waste you. My God wants good for all. It is simple logic. If He has instilled love within parents for all their children, then He, being the Parent of all parents, wants good for all by priority. If my God wants good for me, then He wants good for all, and if He wants salvation for me, then He wants salvation for all. So then how can my God allow me to condemn you, and how can your God allow you to condemn me? This would mean our God is inconsistent. Is God inconsistent, or is it our thinking about God that is inconsistent? Is the way in which we have interpreted our God and His communication inconsistent, or is God Himself inconsistent?

A disciple said to one of our later Imams, "I am the assistant of a philosopher who is writing a treatise on discrepancies in the Quran." The Imam said, "When he finishes writing it, come to me and I shall pose a question, which you can then ask the philosopher." Upon completing the book, the philosopher said to his assistant, "Here is the book. Soon it shall be within the public domain, and everyone will see that there are inconsistencies within the Quran." The disciple went to the Imam as instructed, and the Imam taught him to ask the following question: "Are these discrepancies within the Quran, or are these discrepancies in your understanding of the Quran?'" The disciple returned to the philosopher and said, "I have a question for you: Are these discrepancies in the mind of God, or are these discrepancies in your interpretations of God's Words?" The philosopher cast his book into the fire and said, "Indeed it is a worthy question, for how is it possible for God to be inconsistent? By definition, God can never be inconsistent."

Thus, we begin to understand that the problem is not with God. The problem can never be with religion as communicated by God. The problem is inside the minds of the faithful. If you examine religion, it is no different to the human being (or anything else for that matter) insofar as it has an 'essence' and a 'form'. The 'essence' of religion, which is at the heart of all monotheistic religions, is God-orientation and God-centricity throughout life, that is, the meaningful and purposeful life is one which is God-oriented and God-centric. We are supposed to tend to that Beautiful One who is the Peak of our aspirations, and to yearn Him from deep within ourselves and complete ourselves by becoming like Him. This is the 'essence' of religion. The arbitrary and 'formal' features of a religion are its devotional ceremonies, including how to pray, by what name to call Him, and places of pilgrimage etc. They assist in attaining the 'essence', which is God-orientation. The rest of the religious ordinances (relating to human interactions, rights, and duties) are not an 'essential' part of religion. They belong to the human domain in general and are to be formulated in accordance with the growth of 'human nobility' of the collectivity and the continually evolving notion of justice. They are not particular to any religion per se.

Let us explain this further. Do any of the monotheistic religions teach that the killing of innocent souls is good? Do any of them assert that transgression upon others is good? Do they state that lying and stealing are good? None of the religions advocate such immoral actions. All religions declare that being righteous and doing good to others is good. Teachings on morality and virtues are common to all religions and hence provide a platform for interfaith dialogue. In fact, they are part of the 'essential' components of religion insofar as they direct us to God and make us godlike. On the other hand, teachings such as the direction we face during ritual prayers, the places of pilgrimage, and the name we use to call God, differ from one faith to another. These are examples of the 'formal' features of a religion. With respect to the norms and regulations pertaining to the domain of human interactions and rights and duties, all people abide by the socio-economic and political systems of the place of their residence irrespective of whether they belong to a particular faith or not.

Thus, the Quran, Torah, Gospel, and the sacred texts of other religions contain teachings advocating the 'essence', which is to become godly creatures and acquire a virtuous state. Additionally, they prescribe 'formal' instructions on how the individual and collectivity are to devote themselves to God, and how the individuals of a collectivity within a particular societal context are to interact with each other and their environments, in order that they cultivate virtues and attain godliness. If examined objectively, we realise that just as we were deceived early on in our human journey by mistaking the arbitrary and 'formal' features of our bodies and lives as being 'essential', resulting in discrimination against the 'other' based on the imagined superiority of our 'formal' features, the same thing has occurred regarding our attitudes towards other religions: 'I am superior to him because I have the Ka'ba, and he has something different.'

How strange is the outlook of the faithful believer, irrespective of whether he is a Muslim, Jew, Christian or Hindu, for he admits to a God Who stands at the peak of perfection and is uncontainable within the parameters of time and space, and yet he confines Him – that Timeless and Spaceless One – to a particular place and direction? The Quran states:

> *The fools among the people will say, 'What has turned them away from the prayer direction they used to face?' Say, 'The east and west belong to Allah. He guides whomsoever He will to a right path.' (2:142)*

One set of believers confine their God to the Ka'ba, and the other to the great temple. Indeed, He is an unworthy God in that case. On paper, all the faithful assert that He cannot be encompassed by the whole of existence in its entirety, and yet we wish to put Him inside the four walls of the Ka'ba? These things, such as the direction of prayer, were never meant to be considered as 'essential' features of religion. They are the 'formal' parts of religion. They pertain to the realm of the 'bodily' (that is, to time and space) and are necessary for the God-orientation and cohesion of the members of a collectivity.

Similarly, the great men who led virtuous lives, conveyed spiritual and moral teachings, and hence are role models, belong to particular religions from the 'bodily' (or outward) perspective only. Their true belonging is with the 'essence' of religion. The function of their 'bodily' (or outward) role in religion is like any other 'formal' aspect of religion. The faithful of each religion have made the devotional 'forms' and personalities of their particular religion into the *essence* of religion. Consequently, every religion makes the claim to Truth *exclusively* based on their respective 'forms' and personalities, exacerbating the very tendencies within humans that religion came to liberate them from, namely exploitation, corruption, bloodshed, and all the other manifestations of egocentricity. Ironically, religions have managed to bring the worst out in us at times.

Intuitively and through reflection, we know that God cannot be less than perfect, and hence anything that is from God can only make us godly and not ungodly. God is unlimited and unrestricted, beautiful in His entirety. Hence, His communication in the form of religion cannot be restrictive. It is us – the faithful – who have perverted religion by projecting our insecurities, prejudices, and arrogance onto our interpretations of God's Words.

I often ask this question: What makes Husayn 'Husayn'? Is it the label of 'Islam', or is it Imam Husayn's 'essence' and what he stood for? If it is his 'essence' (that is, if it is that the fact that his soul is perpetually centred upon God), then we can remove the formal designation of 'Islam', and Imam Husayn is still the same Imam Husayn. But if Imam Husayn has value only because of the label of 'Islam' (that is, because he performed the 'bodily' rituals and rules of Islam), then without that label, all that Imam Husayn did and stood up for is empty and does not have the same lofty value. Therefore, if Imam Husayn is Imam Husayn by virtue of his own self or God-centred soul, then the label of 'Islam' can be replaced and removed, and Imam Husayn will still be Imam Husayn. The fact that he appeals across faiths shows he transcends the formal faith of Islam and belongs to the 'essence' of religion.

The following illustrates the consequence of conflating the 'forms' of religion with its 'essence': I was invited to take part in the *High-level International Consultation* at the United Nations addressing the issue of "Advancing the Protection of Minorities in Muslim Majority States". We were discussing the rights of minorities within Muslim countries. In today's pluralistic and global community, we are faced with the serious charge of not affording equal rights and opportunities to non-Muslim minorities in Muslim countries. By adhering to formal Islam with respect to the rights of the 'other', or in other words by adhering to the 'letter' of the Sharia law, the most Muslims can offer the 'other' is a form of compromised citizenship to members of the Abrahamic faiths alone, and that too with the proviso of *jizya* (a capitation tax formerly levied on non-Muslims by an Islamic state). This means that people belonging to the non-Abrahamic faiths have 'no status', not even a compromised one. Earlier Muslim generations circumvented the problem by asserting that other faiths were 'essentially' monotheistic and hence were part of the Abrahamic faiths. Now look at the problem: we know intuitively that everyone should have equal rights by virtue of citizenship even in a Muslim state, but because we have mistaken formal Islam for its 'essence', we are stifled. Our understanding of Islam becomes narrow and counterintuitive; we reject what we know to be right intuitively.

Now we had to find a solution, but we could not work outside the texts of Islam. The only option was to find texts that supported our intuition. We know what is right by virtue of the faculty of intuition, and yet religion – or our understanding of it – does not allow for it. So how did we overcome this problem? We had to find Sharia texts and evidences in favour of pluralistic societies. Why could we not have taken a fresh approach? We merely needed to state that the message of God could not be inconsistent with morality, reason, and intuition. Hence, whatever is contrary to them must be a perversion of religion and wrong in the current context. Then we would not need to rummage for Sharia texts and evidences to justify our intuition. Why can we not be bold enough to acknowledge that we have not understood religion? If we can admit this, then we can move towards a solution. To frame the issue differently: what we are witnessing is a conflict between the religion of God that is within us and the 'formal' or 'literal' appreciation of the texts of the religion of God.

When we analyse the evolution of the 'forms' of religion, we find the *sharia* of Prophet Ibrahim was addressing the rational, moral, and spiritual needs of his family and a small group of followers. Consequently, it had very few regulations in addition to emphasising the 'essence' of religion (which is to be God-centric and acquire human virtues). In the case of Prophet Musa and the Israelite community, the *sharia*, or 'form' of religion, was a sophisticated system of ordinances and regulations. It had many more regulations in addition to emphasising the 'essence' of religion. The community of Prophet Musa was akin to a society and hence needed more elaborate and sophisticated regulations, whereas the community of Prophet Ibrahim was akin to a small tribe and hence warranted few regulations.

The 'form' of religion, or Sharia, of Prophet Muhammad was more sophisticated than the 'forms' or *sharias* of previous prophets. This is because his audience was more sophisticated, and had different rational, moral, and spiritual needs. This means the 'form' of religion is contingent upon the sophistication, demands, and needs of the humans it is addressing. Therefore the 'form' of religion revealed to every prophet was different to those revealed to other prophets. It would have been non-sensical for Prophet Ibrahim and his community to have received the Sharia of Prophet Muhammad, and vice versa. The ever-changing human mind and the evolution of 'human nobility' of the collectivity results in the gradual sophistication of human interactions, rights, and responsibilities, which then require corresponding and appropriate societal regulations.

Therefore, religion teaches that the purpose of life (or the good life) is to become God-centric and acquire a virtuous state. This is the 'essence' of religion. The question of 'how do we become God-centred in our context?' was and continues to be in the minds of the followers of prophets. The diverse 'forms' of religion of the different prophets answered this question, and they had to be different. Would you say that the course of study for a child in primary education and the course of study for an adult at postgraduate level must be one and the same? The methods are different, the textbooks are different, the libraries are different, the tutors are different, and the coursework is different; all of it is different, to the extent that even the lifestyle has changed. Similarly, the 'essence' of every religion is the same but their 'forms' differ depending on time, place, and people.

This idea is not an alien idea. In fact, it is a lived existential reality. In certain regions of India, women mature far quicker than European women, and consequently they are given household responsibilities at a significantly younger age. They are the same 'essentially', that is, they are human beings who are supposed to live good lives, but because of differences in their lifestyles, physical and social circumstances, they receive their responsibilities at different ages. In some places, children's aptitudes for learning are far greater than those in other places, and so the education and schooling differ accordingly. No two regions in the world are exactly the same with respect to the physical and psychological development of children; this is also true for people in general. In view of such relativity, religion has had to and must continue to provide appropriate 'forms' of regulations catering for the different circumstances, aptitudes, and mentalities of people in different regions of the world. Thus, 'forms' are context and people-specific. They are not part of the *essence* of religion. It is when the *form* of religion is mistaken for the *essence* of religion that Sharia regulations and theology become problematic.

Therefore, religions are the same *in essence* but differ from one another *in form*. It is just like human beings: they are the same *in essence* but different *in form*. What distinguishes one human from another is the 'form' (that is, the shape, size, and other features of the body and psyche), but what unites us all together is the 'essence'. The same is true for the various religions and sects that govern human life.

This lecture series will examine the notion of religion as per the Quran. According to the Quran, religion is a *perennial* truth given to all the Prophets. The 'essence' of this *perennial* religion, which is God-centricity and the acquisition of human virtues, has been refashioned in differing contexts. The Quran affirms the plurality and diversity of the 'forms' of religion as part of the divine planning. Its attitude towards the 'other' is 'acceptance' and 'integration' as opposed to 'tolerance'. It accepts their truth-claims to a great degree, and respects and tolerates erroneous ones. Thus, the Quran exhorts mutual cooperation and harmonious coexistence between the people of different faiths on the basis of the shared 'essence' (which is God-centricity and the acquisition of human virtues). Hence, the Quran is both pluralistic and inclusivist. It gives equal value to the devotional 'forms' of the Abrahamic faiths. The Quran also alludes to the *mutability* of Sharia regulations, affirming the idea of there being 'no finality' in the fashioning of societal regulations. Accordingly, these lectures will argue that they are to be re-formulated in line with the evolution of our understanding of what is 'just' and 'noble'. Finally, this lecture series discusses soteriology (the doctrine of salvation) as per the Quran. It explores the fact that salvation is possible for every person irrespective of faith, and that the dichotomy of 'the friend of God' and 'the enemy of God' is central to the Quran's discourse on salvation and damnation.

The conflict between the traditional understanding of religion and our intuitions will persist until we go back to the Quran and read it afresh, for it is the core guidance for Muslims unconditionally. Most of us choose to either ignore the conflict outright or suppress the intuitions. Therefore, we need to journey across the Quran – the most eloquent of God's speech – for it will justify our intuitive understanding and give us the confidence to trust our faculties of intuition and reason.

In summary, we know intuitively that humankind is one, that religion has come to remind us of this truth, that God has ordained different religions, and yet He wants goodness for all of us. Thus, we need to work out what the differences are and what is same. The *essence* is the same, and the *forms* are different. Now consider the following questions: Does the Quran make a distinction between 'the Islam of the Muslims' (with uppercase 'I' and 'M') and 'the *islām* of the *muslims*' (with lowercase 'i' and 'm')? What is the relationship between them? Is one of them a 'form' and the other the 'essence'? What does the Quran say about other religions? Does it accommodate them and their beliefs? Or does it state that only 'uppercase Islam' carries the truth? Does the Quran state that all religions are equally correct? In other words, is it pluralistic? Or does it say that other religions are the same at the level of the *essence*, and that the truth is *perennial*?

Think about these things carefully. On the one hand, all religions assert that God is the Beautiful One and the Peak of human aspiration – this is the *essence* of religion. On the other hand, there are the particularities of the different religions, such as 'God has a son', 'God has avatars', and 'God is one, unbounded, and there is nothing like Him'. Now how can we say that all these particularities are equally true? Moreover, how can somebody who believes that God has avatars, or a son, qualify for salvation? Yet the Quran offers the adherents of the other religions salvation despite holding such beliefs, which means that salvation depends upon something beyond the mere correct understanding of the features of God. Salvation depends upon one's subjective or inner relationship with God and how godlike we have become. So, is it possible to say that such beliefs about God are true when we know that God does not have a child or avatars? Of course not, God does not have a son or avatars. Epistemically, these are false assertions. It is here that we can debate rationally, but can we say that a person holding a false notion of God is not godly? No. This is because godliness depends upon an individual relating and growing to the real, intuitively known God, Who is beyond the descriptive and notional God. Perhaps the individual with an erroneous description and notion of God relates to God more intimately than most people in this world, including Muslims, and hence is growing towards Him at a faster rate? These are the kinds of questions we will investigate.

How beautiful is the Imam in whose name we have congregated? These Imams were godly creatures, for they had the prophetic substance of their grandfather, the great Prophet Muhammad; they were profound. In the army of Imam Husayn, some of his followers were praying with their arms folded; it did not concern him. Amongst his killers were those praying with their arms open; it did not prevent Allah from condemning them. Salvation and damnation are not contingent upon the arms being folded or open during prayers. In the army of Husayn, one of his followers is a Christian, another hardly knows him, and another accepts him as the grandson of the Prophet and the son of the fourth *khalī-fa* but not as the son of the first Imam. These particularities are subject to analysis and critique; they may be right or wrong. One person reasons that God does not have a son, and another believes that God has a son; in this case, one is right, and the other wrong. Yet, Imam Husayn understands that there is an area in which all his followers are right. It is the genuine relationship one has with the real and intuitively sensed God that lies beyond all these descriptions, particularities, and notions of God. Imam Husayn sees their genuine love for God and finds them all righteous.

Lecture Two
Diversity of Forms

The purpose of our existence is to serve Allah: "I have not created jinn and humankind except to serve Me." (51:56) Serving Allah has to correspond with the knowledge base Allah has bestowed upon us by virtue of His teaching Adam 'all the names' (see 2:31). In consideration of human history, the successive revelations, and the fact that there is all this potential knowledge within us, 'service to Allah' can only mean surrendering to God and actualising our human potential. We can extrapolate two levels of 'devotion' or 'surrender' to God in the Quran. The first consists of examining nature, discovering its secrets, and utilising it accordingly. These are among the existential facets of humankind (that is, they pertain to its nature): We delve into the oceans uncovering its treasures and penetrate the depths of space displaying our understanding and mastery over the physical laws of nature. At this level, the intention is for us to come of age and begin to mirror the Divine Himself: We become creators and nurturers like Him. To cure, prolong life and dispel poverty are undeniable abilities of our humanity. 'Becoming His vicegerents' (see 2:30) entails actualising the great potential of knowledge within us whereby we care for the earth and all its inhabitants (which includes the mineral, plant, and animal kingdoms) even if we are not explicitly commanded to.

The other level of 'devotion' or 'surrender' to God pertains to our inner world: the soul's psyche and heart. Here, we are required to become focused upon God totally by inner surrender and worship. This entails handing over the ego to God resulting in inner growth and the emergence of His light in and through us.

Therefore, Allah's instruction to serve Him consists of two actions: one is the actualisation of our potential knowledge such that we do His work as His vicegerents, and the other is the realisation of the moral virtues and innate God-centricity in the soul. Ideally, both actions are meant to progress hand in hand, for both are facets of God-centricity.

To reiterate for clarity, if God has not intended for us to progress rationally (that is, in terms of knowledge), then why has He vested us with such tremendous rational potential coupled with an insatiable curiosity? It seems that rational progression and inward surrender to God are invariably connected: As the mind observes the wonders of existence, the heart yields and surrenders to God. In fact, the Quranic exhortations to observe the universe analytically is inextricably connected to the psychological states of wonderment at God's creation and acknowledgment of His mastery. Consider the verse: "Those who remember Allah whilst standing, sitting, and lying down on their sides, and they reflect upon the creation of the heavens and the earth, [and exclaim]: 'Our Lord! You have not created this in vain…'" (3:191). Thus, it seems the scientific/rational understanding of the ecological balance and meticulous workings of the natural world yields greater appreciation of God resulting in inner humility.

Therefore, rational progression and inward surrender to God are two forces, or two aspects of the same force (God-centricity), driving human behaviour, and as such they are equally enjoyed by one and all despite the apparent diversities of religion, culture, and so on.

We observe that rational progress occurs when minds are liberated from restrictive notions and hence empowered to inquire.

For instance, the Arabian Peninsula produced the foremost scientists, anthropologists, thinkers, philosophers, explorers, and so on in the world soon after embracing Islam, resulting in a rational and scientific hegemony lasting for a period of eleven centuries. This was the result of the Quran exhorting the exploration of nature and declaring the nature of the universe to be subservient to humankind (see 67:15 and 31:20), thereby intriguing and empowering the people. This rational progression is also witnessed in the people of faiths prior to Islam and the non-Muslims who came after Islam.

Therefore, the desire to grow rationally is like an instinct inherent in one and all regardless of persuasion; it emerges when the mind is freed from its shackles and allowed to think freely. It should be noted that 'thinking freely' of necessity results in differences of opinion, interpretation, and understanding of facts in the natural world. Such differences are essential parts of the process of constructing knowledge and acquiring greater accuracy of current theories. Finally, all rational progression pertains to the outer component of 'devotion' and 'surrender' to God.

As for the subjective component of 'devotion' and 'surrender' to God, consider the following question: Is not devotion and surrender of the mind and heart to God also equally available to one and all at an existential level, withstanding the diversity of persuasions, the variety of notions of God, and the plurality of methods of attaining the spiritual state?

The Quran states, "There is no compulsion in religion." (2:256) This signifies that inner surrender occurs only by the wholesome acknowledgement of God and the earnest desire to belong to Him. Furthermore, the Quran states, "Had your Lord willed, He could have made humankind into one people, and yet they would not cease differing [with each other about things]." (11:118) Similarly, this verse is stressing that there is no compulsion at an existential level on the part of God, nor any psychological coercion at the level of human consciousness; in other words, God has not created us of one persuasion only, and there is no expectation for us to conform to a particular outlook without our choosing.

Allah has not made us into one people by default; variety and diversity are existential. Individuality and difference are the hallmarks of our existence and creation. Allah says: "Among His signs is the creations of the heaven and the earth and the difference of your languages and your colours. Surely in that are signs for those who know." (30:22) No two people can be the same; even identical twins are not identical in every way physically, let alone psychologically. In terms of sense perception, no two individuals see the same thing in the same way due to differences in the aptitudes of the organs of sense perception, and then no two people interact identically with whatever they apprehend at the level of sense perception; like two people reading the same novel – one is moved to tears, whereas the other is unaffected. Even two people of the same persuasion do not understand God in the same way, nor do they relate to him in an identical manner. These differences are existential, that is, they are engineered by God, and so naturally He affirms them.

Consider the following verse in which God refers to the subjective component of inner surrender in spite of all this difference: "O humankind, We have created you from a male and a female, and made you nations and tribes that you may know each other. Verily, the noblest among you with Allah is the most God-conscious of you. Indeed, Allah is All-knowing, All-aware." (49:13) This is a most striking verse! He is not addressing the Muslims exclusively, nor the believers specifically, and neither is His address restricted to the People of the Book. He is addressing the whole of mankind. He is saying: 'I have made you into different groupings, the purpose of which is for you to interact with each other and learn that there is a common purpose despite your differences. That common purpose is to fully actualise your existence and arrive at the pinnacle of godliness. You may be brown, white, or yellow ¬– these differences are arbitrary and accidental. The *noblest among you* do not fully actualise their existence and arrive at the pinnacle of godliness by virtue of their brownness, whiteness, or yellowness, but by realising their humanity and being godly. You may be a Christian, Hindu, Muslim, Jew, Buddhist, or Sikh – it is of no consequence, because being *the best* depends on your humanity and godliness; it does not depend upon these labels of 'faith'. The *best among you* is the one in whose soul the truth of God resides.'

Allah is being very clear: 'You are all different, yet your origin is the same – in *essence* you are one and the same. Your purpose is to come of age rationally and be God-centric.' These verses state that Allah has deliberately kept things the way they are. Plurality in the broadest sense is an absolute hallmark of existence and we cannot get rid of it: Our features, languages, cultures, and religions are all different – the ways in which we live our lives are different. Even the way each one of us relates to and understands God subjectively within the folds of the same religion or sect is unique.

When the Prophet migrated to Medina, he was faced with the organised Abrahamic monotheistic faiths. The first few verses of Sūra al-Baqara – the second chapter of the Quran and the first chapter to be revealed after the migration – state:

> *This Book in which there is no doubt, is a guidance to the God-conscious, who believe in the Unseen, perform the prayer, and spend of what We have provided them; who believe in what has been revealed to you [O Muhammad] and what was revealed before you, and are certain of the Hereafter. (2:2-4)*

The implication here is that all the revelations of God are one and the same, and that there is no difference between any of them 'essentially'. The differences that set them apart from each other are 'formal' differences, just like our features and cultures that set us apart from each other. They are all from the same God;

hence, the speech of God has to be the same *in essence*. Consider the following verse in which Allah states that He has given specific *sharias* to each group or community of people:

> *We have revealed to you [O Muhammad of] the Book with the truth, as a confirmation of what came before It of the Book, and as a sure witness over it. So judge between them according to what Allah has revealed, and do not follow their whims instead of what has come to you of the truth. We have assigned a law and a path to each of you. If Allah willed, He would have made you one people, but He wanted to test you in what He has given you. So compete [with each other] in good deeds; your return, all of you, is to Allah; and He will inform you of what you used to differ about. (5:48)*

Our Sharia, the Muslim Sharia, consists of dos and don'ts – devotional and societal regulations – we are supposed to adhere to. Thus, God is saying to mankind: 'Had I wanted, I could have made you all the same, but I have decided not to make you all the same. I have made you into different peoples, and I have given different *sharias* to each of you accordingly.' Observe how the verse ends denoting the purpose of this diversity as envisaged by God: "Compete with each other in good deeds." He is saying to his immediate audience – the Christians, Jews, Sabians, and Muslims of Medina: 'I have given different *sharias* to each of you. I have not made you into one people deliberately. Now the aim of this is to test you in accordance with what has been given to each of you, and to see which of you does the best.' He is not preferring a Christian over a Jew, nor a Jew over a Muslim. There is no favouritism towards the Muslim here; all are equal. The eventual return for one and all is to Allah. Therefore, Allah is concerned about the 'essence', which is godliness and goodness, beyond the variety of 'forms' of the different *sharias* and *manāhij* (pl. of *minhāj*, denoting ways, methods, programmes) that He has given to each religious community. The central point of this verse is: go forward in accordance with whatever He has given you and attain the best of yourselves.

Even though the apparent differences in the variety of methods of relating to God do not infringe upon the purpose of attaining human completion at the rational and spiritual levels, nonetheless we have to admit to differences in the epistemic accuracy of claims regarding the nature of God and other theological claims. God refers to these differences in the Quran and asserts the need to accurately verify the truth of all such claims. However, despite the inaccuracy of the theological claims of certain religions and sects, Allah states:

> *[O Believers], do not argue with the People of the Book save in the best manner, except those of them that do wrong; and say, 'We believe in what was revealed to us and in what was revealed to you; our God and your God are one [and the same], and to Him we have surrendered.' (29:46)*

Hence, even these differences do not faulter with the 'essence', which is *God-centricity* and *the acquisition of human virtues*. God acknowledges that one view about the nature of God is accurate, and the other is not: When people say, 'God has a son', they are mistaken in their claim, and you can rationally discuss this point; however, then Allah says: 'Tell them that we believe in everything that has been revealed unto us and everything that has been revealed unto you. Our God and your God is one and the same God.' To reiterate, the verse is saying that we are the same people in essence, for their God and our God is one God. Moreover, we are instructed to express that we believe in whatever has been revealed unto them and whatever has been revealed unto us, for it is one revelation. We are also permitted — should the situation warrant it — to express in the kindest possible manner that they have interpreted their revelation in a manner that is not accurate. However, this inaccuracy in the interpretation of their own revelation does not deserve condemnation at all, because salvation depends only on the 'essence', which is God-centricity and the acquisition of human virtues, as per the previous verse, and we shall demonstrate this further in due course.

In summary, Allah does acknowledge that there are certain misinterpretations about the nature of God, and hence we are allowed to discuss rationally with the people of other religions about the nature of God: whether He is one and has avatars or children, or not. However, at a more fundamental level, we are all the same, for we are all serving the same God, and we are all trying to understand the same revelation albeit in different 'forms'.

Recall when the Christians visited the blessed Prophet. During their conversation, they claimed that Prophet Isa was the son of God. Their main argument was based on the fact that Prophet Isa was not conceived via the agency of a human father. Allah responds in a simple and logical manner: "Indeed, the case of Isa in Allah's sight is like the case of Adam: He created him from dust, then He said to him, 'Be!', and he was." (3:59) Now, if you are claiming that Isa is 'the son of God' because he was conceived without a human father, then Adam was created independently of both a father and a mother, and so you have to admit that Adam, by priority, has a greater claim to be 'the son of God'. However, since being created independently of both a father and a mother is not a sufficient reason for you to acknowledge Adam as 'the son of God', then, by priority, you cannot claim Isa to be 'the son of God' on the basis of him being conceived without a human father. Then Allah commands the blessed Prophet to challenge the Christians: 'If you are not going to accept this rational argument, then let us invoke Allah to imprecate the false ones.' ("And whoever disputes with you concerning him (Isa) after the knowledge that has come to you, say: 'Come, let us call our sons and your sons, our women and your women, our selves and your selves, then let us humbly pray and invoke Allah's curse upon the liars.'" – 3:61) They did not engage in the challenge, and yet

Allah honoured them – He allowed them to remain Christians and practice their faith. They failed to defend their belief both rationally and spiritually, and yet their attachment to their method of surrender and devotion to Allah (that is, via Isa as 'the son of God') was so firm, that they could not let it go and convert.

Consider the following verse: "Say [O Muhammad], O People of the Book, you are upon nothing until you establish the Torah and the Gospel." (5:68) If Allah did not value the People of the Book as they were, and if He did not see any efficacy in their *sharias* and paths, then He would not have exhorted them to "establish the Torah and Gospel" in order to be on solid grounds. Here, Allah is not merely confirming that He has given them their own *sharias* and paths, He is also affirming that their *sharias* and paths are efficacious, which means that their Books have value and truth. Allah is telling them: 'You are not on solid grounds until you establish the Torah and Gospel, but once you do *that*, then you qualify as firm believers in whatever I have given you.' Allah is stating this despite any theological perversions and wrong notions of God they may believe in.

In view of the diversity and plurality of religious beliefs, *sharias*, and paths in Medina, the Quran states:

> *"Say, 'O People of the Book, let us come to a statement that is common between us and you, that we serve none but Allah, and that we do not associate anything with Him, and that none of us takes others as lords beside Allah.' And if they turn their backs [from you O Muhammad and believers], say: 'Bear witness that we are Muslims.'" (3:64)*

The Quran is exhorting interfaith dialogue and cooperation. This verse is an example of the inclusivism, pluralism, and tolerance of the Quran towards members of other faiths. When we reflect upon such verses, we realise that Allah is admitting to the simultaneous existence of diversity and commonalities among the Abrahamic faiths.

The Quran has a variety of outlooks towards the monotheistic faiths. Regarding 'forms' of devotion, the Quran institutes 'forms' of devotion for the followers of the blessed Prophet Muhammad specifically, and it expresses an attitude of *pluralism* towards the 'forms' of devotion of the other faiths. As regards the theological beliefs of the different organised faiths (pertaining to the nature of God, creation, and other theological issues), the Quran offers the most precise understanding of the nature of God, His creation, and other theological issues for believers to internalise, and it portrays an attitude of *inclusivism* towards the belief systems of other faiths: that is, they are all true but to a lesser degree. This is because the most fundamental of beliefs – namely the Oneness of God and the contingency of His creation – are upheld by the other faiths despite some of their other beliefs being false (such as the notion of the Trinity in Christianity). In fact, the Quran depicts an attitude of *tolerance* towards members of other faiths with respect to their false beliefs, as in the case of the event of *Mubahila*, despite its attitude of epistemic *exclusivism* regarding the Oneness of God and the contingency of His creation.

Finally, the Quran emphasises the *individual's relationship to God* as central and fundamental to soteriology and salvation as opposed to the individual's membership to any particular faith. In other words, salvation depends exclusively on the subjective or personal relationship of the individual soul to God irrespective of any particular faith: "Indeed, those who believe (that is, the followers of the Prophet Muhammad), and the Jews, Sabians, and Christians, whoever [amongst them] has faith in Allah and the Last Day and does good deeds, they shall have no fear, nor shall they grieve." (2:62) Allah refers to these four faiths specifically because they seem to have been established in Medina; other faiths must not have had a significant presence and hence are not mentioned. The phrase, "those who believe", refers to individuals following the instructions and guidance of the Prophet Muhammad. At the time of the revelation of this verse, the word *muslim* did not refer to them (that is, they were not yet being referred to as 'Muslim'), just as the word *islām* was not yet being used to refer to their faith (or the religion of 'Islam'). God places all these faiths on an equal footing and promises salvation to all who have faith in Allah and the Last Day, and perform righteous deeds. He does not give preference to "those who believe" (in the message of the Prophet Muhammad) over the Jews, or to the Jews over the Christians or Sabians. He is saying: 'Despite all the formal 'labels' or designations you have for the organised faiths you belong to, whomsoever among all of you believes in Allah and the Last Day, and does righteous deeds, they will have their reward and no fear shall befall them, nor shall they grieve.' (See 2:62)

In summary, this verse (in addition to the other verses discussed previously) makes it clear that the Quran views the truth as *perennial*, the expressions (or 'forms') of the truth as *plural*, and salvation as *individual*. It acknowledges the singularity of the source of origin of these faiths and the salvific nature of their spirituality. To reiterate, salvation is a subjective affair of the hearts. This means that despite all the diverse interpretations found in the religions of God (and undoubtedly some are more accurate than others), salvation depends solely on an *individual's* subjective or inner surrender to God, irrespective of faith, religion, or sect. In other words, salvation is entirely dependent upon an *individual's* relationship and bonding with God beyond the 'formal' theology of any religion (see 26:89).

Now does the Quran restrict the possibility of the inner component of surrender (upon which salvation depends), and the outer component of rational completion, to the followers of the faiths of the People of the Book and nobody else? The answer is 'no'. Consider the following verse: "O humankind, We have created you from a male and a female, and made you nations and tribes that you may know each other. Verily, the noblest among you with Allah is the most God-conscious of you. Indeed, Allah is All-knowing, All-aware." (49:13) This verse addresses the entirety of humankind. It is not limiting its address to any one faith or a set of faiths. The *sūra* was revealed in the ninth year after the migration, that is, very late in the Medinan period. At this point in time, the Muslims had expanded their territories considerably. Allah is stating, 'those of you most honoured by Us are the God-conscious irrespective of race and tribe', which means regardless of language, culture, religions, and sects. In other words, this verse is emphasising that salvation is a possibility for all individuals.

The pluralism, inclusivism, and individualism of the Quran do not sit well with today's traditional Muslim theologian who counters by citing 'exclusivist' verses apparently abrogating the verses offering the possibility of salvation to all individuals, including those of other faiths. This theme has been discussed in last year's lectures (which have also been published), but due to its relevance here, we will discuss it again with more depth and clarity.

Firstly, one would think quite naturally that upon achieving strength, success, and domination in the final years of blessed Prophet's mission, Islam would be magnanimous and demonstrate greater tolerance towards diversity and the other faiths; however, according to today's traditional scholars, Islam was magnanimous and demonstrated tolerance towards diversity and other faiths only at its inception, and upon succeeding and gaining strength and domination, it became absolutely *exclusivist* and intolerant. Now, to any thinking mind, this is tantamount to deception and hypocrisy on the part of God and his Prophet. This is because, according to today's traditional scholars, those verses stating that salvation depends upon the individual's inner commitment to God irrespective of faith, religion or sect were never really serious about granting salvation to the members of other faiths, religions or sects. In other words, God knew all along that He was going to abrogate those verses towards the end of the revelatory period, and so He and the blessed Prophet were merely appeasing the members of other faiths to create a favourable attitude towards the Muslims for the time it was expedient.

Now consider the verse of Sūra al-Tawba – the penultimate chapter to be revealed – usually cited by today's traditional scholars to counter other verses offering the possibility of salvation to one and all: "Fight those amongst the People of the Book who do not [truly] have faith in Allah and the Last Day, and do not forbid what Allah and His Messenger have forbidden, and do not follow 'the religion of the Truth', ¬until they pay the tax readily and are subdued." (9:29) On the face of it, this verse seems to be abrogating all previous verses acknowledging the validity of the other *sharias* and professing the possibility of salvation for one and all irrespective of religion, faith, or sect, that is, it seems to be giving the impression of *exclusivism*.

Contrast this verse with the earlier verse stating that salvation is possible for members of the Abrahamic faiths: "Indeed, those who believe (that is, the followers of the Prophet Muhammad), and the Jews, Sabians, and Christians, whoever [amongst them] has faith in Allah and the Last Day and does good deeds, they shall have no fear, nor shall they grieve." (5:69) This verse asserts that merely belonging to the group formally designated as "those who believe" is not of any consequence unless the individual has actual faith in God and the Last Day beyond *formally* belonging to the religion of the Prophet Muhammad. To think, "I am Muslim by birth", is of no significance to God, but to acknowledge God individually and personally from the depths of one's soul, and then to engage in righteous work, is something of merit. The verse says that this is also the case for the Jew, Christian, and Sabian as well. Therefore, being a 'Muslim' in and of itself does not automatically qualify an individual for salvation according to this verse.

Now the verse in Sūra al-Tawba (9:29) only refers to "those amongst the People of the Book who *do not [truly] have faith* in Allah and the Last Day...", whereas the earlier verse from Sūra al-Mā'ida (5:69) is addressing only "... those amongst 'those who believe', the Jews, Sabians, and Christians who *have faith in Allah and the Last Day*...". The distinction is clear: one verse is referring to those who *have faith* among the People of the Book, whereas the other is addressing those who *do not have faith* among the People of the Book. In other words, the verse of Sūra al-Tawba is not referring to all the People of the Book and asserting that they are all unbelievers; it is merely addressing those among them who do not believe. Thus, there is no conflict between the verses, and so there is no sense in claiming the abrogation of one by the other. In fact, according to the principle in these verses (that salvation depends on an individual truly having faith in God and the Last Day), the Muslim who does not truly have faith in God and the Last Day inwardly, and does not do good works, will not attain salvation.

Moreover, the context of the verse of Sūra al-Tawba is the forthcoming battle between the Muslims and groups of Christians. Thus, its tone is one of spurring the Muslims into battle; hence, the verse emphasises fighting until they submit and pay the *jizya* (the tax for non-Muslims). As for the segment of the verse stating "… and [those who] do not abide by 'the religion of the Truth'…", the expression 'the religion of the Truth' is not referring to the 'formal' stipulations of Islam, as shall be explained in later discussions on the notion of *dīn* (religion) in which we will demonstrate, if God so wills, that societal norms of the Sharia are in a state of flux and 'no-finality'.

Consider the following verse: "He it is Who sent His Messenger with guidance and 'the religion of the Truth', that He might cause it to prevail over all [other 'forms' of] religion, though the polytheists may be averse." (9:33) The previous verse ends with the phrase, "*though the unbelievers are averse*". ("They desire to put out the light of Allah with their mouths, and Allah refuses [for that to happen] but rather [He wills] that He completes His light, though the *unbelievers* are averse." 9:32) Today's traditional scholar interprets both verses to mean that everybody will eventually become Muslim and follow Islam, and hence there will only be one religion in the world. However, this is not the meaning of 'the religion of the Truth' (*dīn al-ḥaqq*), as we shall observe in forthcoming lectures. This verse was revealed in the context of the Prophet, and it is making a prediction about 'the religion of the Truth' in relation to the disbelievers and polytheists of his time. It is a historical fact that the prediction was proven true, for 'the religion of the Truth' did indeed prevail over the religion of the polytheists and disbelievers throughout the region during the lifetime of the Prophet. Now the fact that the prediction (of the prevalence of 'the religion of the Truth') was understood by the Prophet and his followers to have occurred in spite of the other Abrahamic faiths being established alongside the Muslims proves that we are misinterpreting the verse. It should be noted that the word 'polytheists' (*mushrikūn*) refers to the pagan Arabs of Mecca whose unjust and indecent way of life was justified by their religion. The term 'disbelievers' (*kuffār*) was used to refer to people who did not believe in God or the afterlife and to various groups of polytheists who rejected the message of the Prophet despite knowing its truth. The meanings of these terms were discussed to some extent in book three of this series, but we will explore them further in these lectures.

For now, consider the following verse:

Allah said, 'O Isa, I will take you and make you ascend to Me and purify you of those who disbelieve and make those who follow you above those who disbelieve till the Day of Resurrection. Then to Me is your return [all of you], and I will judge between you concerning that in which you differed. (3:55)

God has ordained the survival of Christianity till the Day of Qiyāma. It may be objected that this verse merely states the continuation of the belief in Isa till the Day of Qiyāma and not the continuation of Christianity, and so it is possible the phrase "those who follow you" is referring to the Muslims. Now if we accept this interpretation (for arguments sake), we still face the problem of this verse affirming the continuation of disbelief (*kufr*) till the Day of Qiyāma because it states: "I will make those who follow you, O Isa, superior to those who disbelieve till the Day of Qiyāma …". How naïve is the belief that everybody is going to convert to Islam when God Himself states that the plurality of 'forms' is the nature of His Design and has been decreed until the Blowing of the Trumpet?

In another verse, the Quran states: "There is not one of the People of the Book but will assuredly believe in him [Isa] before his death, and on the Resurrection Day he will be a witness against them." (4:159) This verse declares that all the People of the Book will believe in Isa as the messenger of God prior to their own deaths. If it is speculated that the verse implies (somehow) that everyone will be Muslim in the interim between his return and the Day of Judgement, and so everyone will believe in Isa's messengership, then such an interpretation has two implications: firstly, that the Abrahamic faiths will endure until he returns; and secondly, that the verse had neither any relevance nor significance at the time of its revelation, and hence for God to challenge the People of the Book of Medina with this verse was meaningless at the time.

Verses in Sūra al-Yūsuf narrate the incident when Prophet Yusuf took his brother Binyamin into his custody in accordance with the customs of the king of Egypt: "… He [Yusuf] could not have taken his brother according to 'the *dīn* of the king' except that Allah willed [it]…" (12:76) Obviously, Prophet Yusuf did not worship idols, and so the phrase "the religion (*dīn*) of the king" can only mean the socio-political system of Egypt. Likewise, verses predicting the prevalence of 'the religion (*dīn*) of the Truth' mean the prevalence of its socio-economic and political setup in that time and place. It has nothing to do with the cessation of all plurality and diversity of faiths and religions. We will discuss this matter in greater detail later.

The Quran addresses religions or sects asserting *exclusivism* of the truth and salvation, that is, it responds to claims that the truth and salvation is confined to just one particular religion or sect. It refers to the *exclusivist* claims of some of the Jews and Christians of Medina: "And they say, 'Be Jews or Christians and you shall be guided.' Say [O Prophet]: 'No, rather [ours is] the creed (*milla*) of Ibrahim, a *ḥanīf*; he was not of the polytheists.'" (2:135) The Quran counters the *exclusivist* claims of those Christians and Jews by stating that the truth and salvation lie in upholding the Unity of God and worshipping none other than Him; in other words, only the monotheism of Ibrahim is accurate at an epistemic level.

The Quran also counters the claim of *salvific exclusivism* of some of the Jews and Christians of Medina: "And they say, 'None shall enter Paradise except one who is a Jew or a Christian.' Such are their fancies. Say: 'Produce your proof if you are truthful.'" (2:111) Allah asks them to produce their evidence, and then He states: "Nay, but whoever surrenders his whole self to Allah, and he is doer of good, he has his reward with his Lord; and there is no fear upon them, nor shall they grieve." (2:112) Therefore, the only requirement for salvation is inner belief in God and the performance of righteous deeds; belonging to a particular religion or sect is not important in itself. This has been repeated in many other verses of the Quran, some of which we have already discussed.

Here is yet another instance of the Quran addressing *salvific exclusivism* and the arrogance accompanying it: "They (some of the Jews of Medina) say, 'The Fire will not touch us except for a [few] numbered days.' Say, 'Have you made a covenant with Allah, for Allah never breaks His covenant? Or are you saying about Allah that which you do not know?'" (2:80) Some of the Jews of Medina were making an *exclusivist* claim, and Allah takes issue with this attitude and questions them: 'Are you sure about this claim of yours? Have you taken a pledge from Me? Or are these just claims you are making about Me and My actions without knowledge?' Often, we Muslims fall into the trap of *exclusivism* and make such *exclusivist* claims. Immediately after this verse, Allah says: "Truly, whoever earns evil and is surrounded by his sins, those are the inhabitants of the Fire; they will abide therein. And those who believe and perform righteous deeds, those are the inhabitants of the Garden; they will abide therein." (2:81-82) Again, the Quran's response is universal: salvation is for *anyone* who believes and does righteous deeds irrespective of faith, religion, or sect. It invalidates all exclusivist claims.

Finally, consider the following verse of the Quran which is Allah's response to the Muslims, Jews, and Christians of Medina regarding their *exclusivist* claims of superiority over each other:

> *It will not be in accordance with your desires [O Muslims], nor those of the People of the Book (that is, the Jews and Christians); whoever does evil will have the recompense thereof, and he will not find any protector or helper besides Allah. And whoever does good deeds, male or female, and he [or she] is a believer, these shall enter Paradise, and they will not be wronged the dint in a date-stone. And who has a better religion than he who submits his whole self to Allah, and he is the doer of good [to others] and follows the faith of Ibrahim, a ḥanīf? And Allah took Ibrahim as a friend. (4:123-5)*

All these verses clearly demonstrate that the truth is *perennial*, and salvation is *individual* and pertains to the 'essence'.

In conclusion, the Quran does not view diversity in a negative way. On the contrary, it affirms its necessity as part of Allah's design. It states explicitly that He has made these differences and He has given us different paths to follow; however, in *essence* the aim of all of them is the same, which is to become godly and attain His salvation. The Quran is quick to condemn those who think that they are 'the right ones' and everybody else is wrong. It is categorical that salvation is not dependent upon membership to a particular religion or sect, rather it is only contingent upon God-centricity and the performance of righteous deeds. Finally, the rational actualisation of the human potential and the acquisition of a virtuous state – which are the purposes of our creation as the 'vicegerents' (*khulafā'*) of Allah – are common to humankind at large. It should be noted that the actualisation of the rational potential within every human is possible at the exclusion of the belief in God, whereas the acquisition of a virtuous spiritual state is contingent upon faith in God.

Lecture Three
Religious Exclusivism

We believe that Islam is the only religion resulting in favourable effects in the Hereafter, that we – the Muslims – are the chosen and righteous people and hence salvation is *exclusively* for us, and that everyone else is wrong and worthy of hellfire. The root of this *exclusivist* belief (which is held by many members of each of the different religions, faiths, and sects) ¬is our human bodily condition as indicated in the first lecture, and subsequently we justify it by our interpretations of religious texts. We will examine those verses of the Quran commonly cited by today's traditional Muslim scholar to justify this *exclusivist* position.

Today's traditional scholars cite the following three verses to justify religious *exclusivism*:

- "Indeed, the religion (*dīn*) with Allah is *islām*." (3:19)

- "And whoever desires a religion (*dīn*) other than *islām*, it will never be accepted from him; and in the Hereafter he will be one of the losers (that is, of those who have lost all spiritual good)." (3:85)

- "This day, I have perfected your religion (*dīn*) for you, and I have completed My blessing upon you, and I have chosen for you Islam as a religion (*dīn*)." (5:3)

The case may seem to be clear and definitive upon reading these three verses in isolation of the rest of the Quran and in particular the other verses pertaining to the same issue: the only true religion is Islam, and no other path or religion is acceptable other than Islam, for it is the only path and the only righteous way. However, when we analyse these three verses with other relevant verses, we realise that the Quran's perspective is very different and in fact contrary to our *exclusivist* one.

Assume that Islam is the only religion capable of giving us salvation in the Hereafter, and that this *exclusivism* is due to it being fully completed by God. I would like to pose some questions to the two billion Muslims: Which one of your interpretations of Islam is the correct one? Are you all going to be admitted into Paradise, in which case it does not matter whether you are a Sunni, Shia, Ismaili, Bohra or Salafi? Why then do you fight and kill each other on the basis of the *exclusivity* of your own respective versions of Islam? If you assert that Islam is the final and only accurate religion, and it alone is able to lead to salvation, then why do you charge each other with falsity? (The Muslims go as far as condemning each other to Hell.)

On the other hand, if you say that all of you are guaranteed salvation by virtue of being Muslim despite your differences, then in that case you are admitting to plurality or sectarian *pluralism*. This is because none of you agree about the accuracy of the other's interpretation of Islam and yet all of you are asserting that all Muslims are destined for Paradise. Now, if this is what you are saying, then it should not make any difference to a Shia if they become a Salafi, which of course does not make any sense because they passionately believe that only their interpretation of Islam is correct, and all the others are wrong. Similarly, it will not make any difference to a Salafi if they become a Shia, which does not make sense because they passionately believe that only their interpretation is correct, and all the others are wrong. This thought experiment shows that there is a deep problem in the Muslim mind, a state of crisis in our *exclusivist* thinking; it indicates that *exclusivism* is irrational at its core.

A point to note before discussing this topic: We need to remember that the chronological order of the chapters (*sūras*) of the Quran is different to the order of the chapters of the compiled Quran. For instance, Sūra al-Baqara (the chapter of the Cow) is the second chapter of the compiled Quran, whereas it was the eighty-seventh chapter to be revealed some thirteen years after the commencement of revelation. Likewise, some of the very first chapters to be revealed in Mecca are found at the very end of the compiled Quran. The lack of consideration for the chronology of the Quran is in part causing confusion in our appreciation of certain theological themes in the Quran. The current debate is one such theme.

The term *islām* and its other verbal and nominal derivatives are used in different senses in the Quran. This is very clear when we read the Quran chronologically, whereas the reader is more likely to overlook this when reading the compiled order. In certain verses, the term *islām* is being used in an 'essential' manner, that is, in the sense of a *perennial* truth and phenomenon; however, when these same verses are read in the compiled order, we are likely to mistakenly assume that the term *islām* is referring to formal Islam, after which the other words in these verses give the sense of *exclusivism* to what we have understood the term *islām* to mean.

It must be understood that Islam as a 'formal' faith (or an organised religion) was in the process of being delivered during the revelatory period. Hence, Allah uses the term *mu'minīn* ('believers' or 'faithful') and its verbal derivatives to refer to the followers of Prophet Muhammad's teachings for most of the revelation. Allah only uses the terms *islām* and *muslim* to refer to 'the formal organised religion' and 'the followers of the blessed Prophet' respectively after these new meanings were firmly associated with these two terms in the minds of the people of Medina, and they began to use them in these new senses predominantly. Consequently, we find very few verses in which the terms *islām* and *muslim* refer to 'the organised formal religion' and 'the followers of the blessed Prophet' respectively. In most verses of the Quran – that is, for the entirety of the Meccan period and the majority of the Medinan period – Allah uses the terms *islām* and *muslim* to mean 'surrendering to the will of God' and 'the one who surrenders to the will of God' respectively (and not 'the organised formal religion' and 'the follower of an organised faith').

To reiterate, consider the following verse: "O you who believe (believers)! Believe in Allah…" (4:136). Here, the phrase "O you who believe (believers)" is a formal designation or label for the followers of Prophet Muhammad, whereas the command "Believe in Allah…" is exhorting them to internalise the belief in God with conviction. Similarly, in the verse "O you who believe (believers), … do not die save as *muslims*" (3:102), the phrase "O you who believe (believers)" is a designation for the followers of the Prophet, and the command to "not die save as *muslims*" is exhorting them 'to have true faith and surrender to God'. The Quran uses the words *muslim* and *mu'min* in this way – that is, to mean 'one surrendering to God' and as a formal designation for 'the followers of the teachings of Prophet Muhammad' respectively – in the early and middle period of the revelation. In these periods, the words *muslim* and *islām* were unrelated to the formal religion of the blessed Prophet and his followers. The meanings of the words *muslim* and *mu'min* are reversed in the latter period when the associated meaning of the word *islām* and its derivatives changed in the minds of the audience from 'surrendering to God' to the formal designation for the organised religion of the Prophet. In this latter period, the word *īmān* and its derivatives had the connotation of 'deep faith and conviction'. For instance, consider the following verse: "The Bedouins say, 'we have deep-seated faith (*īmān*) [in Allah]'. Say [O Muhammad], 'You do not have deep-seated faith (*īmān*), but rather [you should] say [O Bedouins], 'we have embraced Islam', for deep-seated faith (*īmān*) has not yet entered within your hearts…'." (49:14) Here, the word *islām* is used as a formal designation for the religion of the Prophet and the word *īmān* is used in the sense of 'deep-seated faith'. We will discuss this verse in more depth later. The exact meanings of the words *islam, muslim, īmān,* and *mu'min* in any given verse is determined by situating the verse in the time, place, or period of its revelation (that is, by situating the verse in its specific context). However, as a general rule, the word *muslim* in the latter period of the revelation was used as a formal designation for one who accepted *islam* in the sense of the formal organised religion of the Prophet, and the word *īmān* and its derivatives were used in the sense of 'deep seated faith and conviction in God'. In contrast to this, their usage in the previous periods of the revelation were the opposite: *islam* and its derivatives had the connation of 'surrendering to God', and *mu'min* and its derivatives were used as formal designations for the followers and teachings of Prophet Muhammad. This will become clearer during this lecture.

Now consider the verses often cited by today's traditional scholar to justify the exclusivist position:

> *Indeed, the religion (dīn) with Allah is islām. Those to whom the Book had been given did not differ except after knowledge had come to them, out of envy among themselves; and whoever denies the communications of Allah, then surely Allah is quick in reckoning. (3:19)*

> *And whoever desires a religion (dīn) other than islām, it will never be accepted from him; and in the Hereafter he will be one of the losers (that is, of those who have lost all spiritual good). (3:85)*

Sūra Āl-Imrān is one of the first chapters (*suras*) to be revealed in Medina. It was revealed during the third year after the migration. At this time, devotional and societal regulations were still being ordained and instituted for the followers of the blessed Prophet, and as such were far from complete. The expressions 'believers' (*mu'minūn*) and 'those who believe' (*alladhīna āmanū*) were understood by the people of Medina to be referring to 'the followers of the Prophet' at this point in time, and so the verses of this *sūra* employ them too. This means that the word *muslim* was not being used at this time to refer to 'the followers of the Prophet', and the word *islām* was not being used to refer to 'the organised formal religion'. To reiterate, the notion of an organised formalised religion known as '*islām*' did not firmly exist at this time, and so the word *islām* in these verses did not refer to 'the formal organised religion', like Christianity or Judaism. Rather, the word *islām* in these verses meant 'surrendering to the will of Allah', which was the *perennial* message given to every previous prophet.

Therefore, the statement "Indeed, the *dīn* with Allah is *islām*" (3:19) is addressing the community of the Prophet, and it conveys that 'surrendering to the will of God and to whatever He has revealed' is acceptable to Allah. This meaning (of the word *islām*) is both consistent with and verified by the previous verse: "Allah bears witness that there is no god but He – and [so do] the angels and those who have knowledge – upholding justice; there is no god but He, the All-Mighty, the All-Wise." (3:18) Furthermore, Allama Tabataba'i states in his exegesis of the Quran that the meaning of *islām* in this verse is 'surrendering to the will of God'.

Thus, the word *islām* in these verses does not refer to '*islām*' which is the fully packaged religion; rather, it means 'surrendering to the will of God'. Henceforth, to distinguish between these two senses of the word '*islām*', the italicised word '*islām*' with lowercase 'i' will refer to 'surrendering to the will of God', and the non-italicised word 'Islam' with uppercase 'I' will refer to 'the organised formalised religion'. Accordingly, the italicised word '*muslim*' with lowercase 'm' will refer to a practitioner of *islām* (that is, 'one surrendering to the will of God'), and the non-italicised word 'Muslim' with uppercase 'M' will refer to a member of formal Islam.

It must be remembered that 'surrendering to the will of God' includes surrendering to whatever He has revealed. This is self-evident, but it is also implied in the portion of the verse after the statement 'Indeed, the *dīn* with Allah is *islām*': "Those to whom the Book had been given did not differ except after knowledge had come to them, out of envy among themselves; and whoever denies the communications of Allah, then surely Allah is quick in reckoning." (3:19) This portion of the verse either indicates that many of the People of the Book in Medina knew that what was being revealed was from God, and hence they were expected to surrender to it and not reject it, or is talking of the earlier scriptures when they were revealed to their respective communities.

This understanding of the word *islām* and *dīn* is also corroborated by the last verse of Sūra al-Kāfirūn, the eighteenth chapter to be revealed in the early part of the Meccan period: "You have your religion (*dīn*), and I have my religion (*dīn*)." (109:6) At the time of the revelation of this verse, the religion was very far from being completed obviously, and so the question arises as to what this 'religion' (*dīn*) of the Prophet was? The only response is: 'surrendering to God and whatever was being revealed from God'. Hence, the terms *islām* and *dīn* mentioned in these verses refer to 'the inward act of surrendering to the will of God'. They do not refer to the organised formal faith of 'Islam' that one belongs to or is a member of.

The second verse from Sūra Āl-Imrān (mentioned above) often cited by today's traditional scholar to justify the exclusivity of formal Islam is: "And whoever desires a religion (*dīn*) other than islām, it will never be accepted from him." (3:85) Again, the 'islām' being referred to in this verse is *islām*, that is, 'surrendering to the will of God and whatever is being revealed', and not 'Islam', the formal organised religion. Consider the previous verse:

Say [O Muhammad], 'We believe in Allah and in what has been revealed to us, and what was revealed to Ibrahim, Ismail, Ishaq, Yaqub and the Tribes, and in what was given to

*Musa, Isa, and the prophets from their Lord. We do not make
a distinction between any of them (that is, the prophets), and
we are surrendered (muslimūn) to Allah.' (3:84)*

Based on the content of this verse and the context of Sūra
Āl-Imrān discussed above, it is clear that the word 'muslimūn'
refers to lowercase *muslims*, that is, 'those trying to surrender to
the will of God and whatever has been revealed to the prophets'.
It does not refer to formal Muslims. Furthermore, since verse
3:84 is part of the semantic context for verse 3:85, and since the
word 'muslimūn' (in verse 3:84) is being used in the sense of *muslims*, then this further corroborates that the words 'islām' and *dīn*
in verse 3:85 are being used in the sense of lowercase *islām*. Thus,
the verse "And whoever desires a religion (*dīn*) other than *islām*, it
will never be accepted from him." (3:85) means that paths other
than 'the path of surrender to God' (*islām*) will never be acceptable to God.

Consider the following verse: "Indeed, those who believe
(that is, the followers of Prophet Muhammad), and the Jews,
Sabians, and Christians, whoever [amongst them] has faith in
Allah and the Last Day and does good deeds, they shall have no
fear, nor shall they grieve." (5:69) This verse is a part of Sūra
al-Māʾida, the antepenultimate chapter, revealed at the end of
the sixth year or the beginning of the seventh year of the migration; hence, it was revealed after Sūra Āl Imrān. At this point
in time, an organised 'formal' religion had formed around the
Quran and Prophet's teachings, and the people of Medina were
using the word 'islām' to refer to it. Thus, the associated meaning
of the word 'islām' had changed from 'surrendering to the will of
God' (*islām*) to 'the organised formal religion' (Islam) by this time.
The same verse with a slight variation was revealed earlier in Sūra
al-Baqara, the first chapter to be revealed in Medina and hence
prior to Sūra Āl Imrān:

Indeed, those who believe (that is, the followers of Prophet Muhammad), and the Jews, Christians, and Sabians, whoever [amongst them] has faith in Allah and the Last Day and does righteous deeds, they will have their reward with their Lord, and there is no fear for them, nor shall they grieve. (2:62)

The repetition of the content of verses in both Sūra al-Māʾi-da and Sūra al-Baqara means that Allah promised salvation to the God-conscious among the Jews, Christians, and Sabians both before and after the existence of formal 'Islam'. This is yet another reason why the term 'islām' in the two aforementioned verses of Sūra Āl Imrān (which were, "Indeed, the *dīn* with Allah is *islām*" (3:19) and "And whoever desires a religion (*dīn*) other than *islām*, it will never be accepted from him." (3:85)) cannot possibly be referring to 'Islam', for otherwise it would be contradicting the promise of God to the God-conscious among the Jews, Christians, and Sabians.

The final verse from Sūra al-Māʾida often cited by today's traditional scholar to justify the *exclusivity* of 'Islam' is: "This day, I have completed your religion (*dīn*) for you, and I have concluded My blessing upon you, and I have chosen for you islām as a religion (*dīn*)." (5:3) This verse was revealed during or after the farewell pilgrimage of the Prophet. In other words, it was revealed in the final stages of revelation. In this verse, the word 'islām' is being used in the sense of uppercase 'Islam'. This is because: firstly, formal 'Islam' is the associated meaning of the word 'islām' in the minds of the people at this point in time; and secondly, the delivery and completion of 'Islam' was almost at hand. We say 'almost' because the regulations of 'Islam' continued being revealed in the Quran and fashioned by the Prophet even after this verse was revealed, as attested to by the exegetes of the Quran.

There are two points to note here: firstly, the word 'islām' had become firmly associated with 'Islam' (the organised 'formal' religion of the Prophet) in the minds of the people towards the end of the revelatory period; and secondly, the regulations of 'Islam' were still being revealed after this verse, that is, despite the verse stating that God had completed 'Islam'. This means the said 'completion' did not include, mean, or refer to the regulations or legal system of 'Islam'.

Moreover, God's usage of the second person plural pronoun (*kum*) is a semantic context limiting the meaning of the word 'islām' to the formal Islam of Muslims: "This day, I have completed *your* religion (*dīn*) for *you*, and I have concluded My blessing upon *you*, and I have chosen for *you* Islam as a religion (*dīn*)." (5:3) This verse is addressing its initial audience thus: 'The religion that you, O Muslims, all belong to and are members of, and which you term as "Islam", has been completed for you to the extent of your requirements.' Otherwise, the verse would have stated: 'I have completed *islām*' or 'I have completed My religion'.

When juxtaposing the other verses using the word 'islām' with this verse emphasising '*you*', '*your* religion', and '*your* Islam', we realise that *islām* is a salient reality acquiring differing 'formal' expressions with the passage and demands of time. This is the reason why the regulations of formal 'Islam' continued being revealed after the conveyance of this verse. Therefore, if it is claimed (on the basis of this verse) that 'Islam' is the final religion, complete and perfect in every way ¬(including its 'formal' aspects), and hence it is the only religion acceptable to God, then one can counter legitimately and genuinely by stating that 'Islam' most definitely was not complete in its 'formal' capacity at the time of the revelation of this verse. This verse is merely announcing to its immediate audience – the Muslims – that the conveyance of *their* formal 'Islam' is drawing to an end, and that alongside the other Abrahamic faiths, it too is salvific by virtue of it being the latest and most up to date version of the same salient religion (*dīn*), which is *islām*.

Therefore, there has only ever been one truth, one religion, one path, or one way; it is the same and has never changed. Allah refers to it as *islām* in the Quran, and it means 'surrendering to the will of God'. Hence, it is not in need of completion. The 'completion' mentioned in Sūra al-Māʾida 5:3 refers to formal 'Islam' generally, that is, its doctrines, ethical outlook, and devotional practices; however, it does not refer to the societal regulations of 'Islam' pertaining to the individual, family, and society for the reason stated above, and also because it is impossible for such regulations to be 'completed' and 'final' in any case, that is, so long as humankind exists in a fluctuating cosmos. This will be discussed in the forthcoming lectures God willing.

So *islām* means 'wilful surrender to Allah', and that is the only '*dīn* with Allah'. This '*dīn* of Allah' has had many expressions throughout the history of humankind, corresponding to the different contexts of peoples: at a particular point in human history, people received the message of *islām* within their own context and decided to call it 'Judaism'; at another point, others received it within their unique context and chose to call it 'Christianity'; and at yet another point, other people received the message of *islām* within their context and called it 'Islam'. Now these 'forms' are all equal as expressions of *islām*. Notice how none of the founders of the subsequent 'forms' of *islām* declared that previous 'forms' were wrong and should be done away with; on the contrary, they affirmed the doctrines, ethical outlooks, and devotional practices of previous 'forms' on the whole and modified them where necessary.

Consider the verse: "And strive hard in [the way of] Allah, [such] a striving as is due to Him; He has chosen you and has not laid upon you a hardship in religion; the creed (*milla*) of your father Ibrahim; He named you *muslim*s before and in this [revelation]..." (22:78) Prior to Prophet Ibrahim, Prophet Nuh was a *muslim* too obviously, however the word 'muslim' did not have a phonetically equivalent word in the languages of his time. By the time of Prophet Ibrahim, the phonetically equivalent ancestor of the Arabic word 'muslim' was part of the proto-Arabic languages which he was accustomed to conversing in (due to his association with the tribe of the Kan'anis). Thus, Allah terms all who surrender to Him alone (and nothing else, such as idols and celestial bodies) from the time of the Prophet Ibrahim onwards as *muslims*.

In Sūra al-Baqara, the Quran states that Ibrahim and Ismail prayed for the following whilst laying the foundations of the Ka'ba: '*Rabbana wa-j'alnā muslimayni laka...*'

> *Our Lord, and make us two muslims for You (two individuals surrendered to You), and from our descendants, [raise] a community who are muslims for You [as well]; and show us our devotional ceremonies, and turn towards us; surely, You are the Oft-Returning, the Most Merciful. Our Lord, and raise up in their midst a messenger from among them who shall recite to them Your communications and teach them the Book and the Wisdom, and purify them; You are the All-Mighty, the All-Wise. (2:128-129)*

Allah responds to Prophet Ibrahim's supplication in 2:131: "*aslim*" ("[O Ibrahim,] surrender"). Ibrahim replied: "*aslamtu li-rabb al-'ālamīn*" ("I have surrendered myself to the Lord of the worlds"). The word *aslim* is an imperative verb meaning 'surrender!', *islām* is a verbal noun signifying 'the state of surrender' or 'the state of having handed oneself over to Allah', and *muslim* is a noun of doership meaning 'one who is surrendering to Allah'.

To summarise, the word 'islām' has two meanings in the Quran: The first is *islām*, which is spiritual orientation to God or the inner state of being surrendered to God, and it is the 'essence' of formal 'Islam'. It is to find God at an intuitive level, that is, finding God deep within, and giving ourselves over to Him. This is the first meaning of the word 'islām' in the Quran. The second meaning of the word 'islām' refers to regulations delivered from time to time to assist people in orienting themselves towards God. These regulations are instructions on *how* to surrender to God and lead a virtuous life in any given context. Accordingly, they comprise of devotional and societal regulations.

The devotional and societal regulations revealed to Prophet Ibrahim were formulated in accordance with the needs of the context of his tribe and few followers; hence, they were minimalistic. They consisted of simple commands and general prescriptions, such as the commands to pray to God and to not kill children, and the prescriptions to not lie, cheat, and deceive; they were neither sophisticated nor detailed. They were perfect for that context for they assisted in the rational, moral, and spiritual growth of both the individual and collectivity. The 'essence' of the religion of Ibrahim (which is 'surrendering to God') continued to be the core of the teachings of subsequent prophets even though the context continued to change gradually, evolving from a small tribe into tribes, then communities, societies, and finally nations. Although the 'essence' of religion remained the same, the devotional and societal regulations formulated for Prophet Ibrahim and his few followers were inadequate in addressing the problems, mentalities, and sophistications of tribes, communities, societies and eventually nations, for each had differing rational, moral, and spiritual needs. Thus, societal regulations had to be adapted to continue to be effective in facilitating the growth of the individual and collectivity towards the 'essence'.

Therefore, regulations change, whereas the 'essence' is salient, universal, and unchanging. In other words, the 'form' is subject to being tweaked and changed as and when the context demands so that it continues to be optimal in facilitating the rational, moral, and spiritual growth of the individual and collectivity. This was understood by the prophets as a self-evident existential truth: when the 'forms' of things change, then the regulations governing them also change accordingly. Hence, older 'forms' of regulations of previous prophets were abrogated by newer 'forms' of regulations of subsequent prophets.

Since the *essence* of religion is *islām*, then anyone who is surrendered to God internally is a *muslim* irrespective of whether the surrender occurs within the folds of the formal religion of

Prophet Muhammad (Islam), Isa (Christianity), or Musa (Judaism). Such individuals are surrendered to God beyond their 'formal' superficial religious identities and theologies, like the prophets of old and some of their followers.

Consider the following verse: "Ibrahim was not a Jew nor a Christian, but he was a *ḥanīf*, a *muslim* (one surrendered to God), and he was not of the polytheists." (3:67) Again, God has used the word 'muslim' in the sense of the *muslim* (that is, one who is surrendered to God internally). Obviously, Prophet Ibrahim was not a formal Muslim like us. To qualify as a formal Muslim, one must believe in the unity of God and the finality of the message (*risāla*) of Prophet Muhammad. How could Prophet Ibrahim believe in the message (*risāla*) of Prophet Muhammad when Prophet Muhammad was not born? So, the question is: How can Prophet Ibrahim be a 'muslim'? What does the Quran mean when it refers to Prophet Ibrahim and other prophets as 'muslims' because they neither accepted the message (*risāla*) of Prophet Muhammad nor followed his Sharia? However, Prophet Ibrahim and the other prophets were *muslims*, that is, they had surrendered to the will of God internally.

The same logic and analysis apply to the following verse of the Quran: "Or were you witnesses when death approached Yaqub, when he said to his sons, 'What will you worship after me?' They said, 'We will worship your God and the God of your fathers, Ibrahim and Ismail and Ishaq – one God; we are muslims unto Him.'" (2:133) Yaqub's children stated that they were 'muslims'. Again, we ask: what type of 'muslim' were they? They were *muslims*. They were declaring that they were among those who surrender to the will of God, and that they do not worship anything other than Him.

The following verse is in Sūra an-Naml:

Then it was said to her [Bilqis], 'Enter the hall,' but when she saw it, she thought it was a pool [of water] and bared her legs. He [Sulayman] said, 'It is just a hall paved with glass.' She said, 'My Lord, I have wronged myself: I surrender (aslamtu) with Solomon to Allah, the Lord of the Worlds.' (27:44)

When Bilqis entered Sulayman's palace, she thought there was a stream flowing beneath her, and so she raised the hem of her garment to prevent it from getting wet. Sulayman told her that the gemstones were creating the illusion of a stream, after which she cried out: "My Lord!..." The promptness and spontaneity of her response shows the deep-seated personal relation she had to God – the One Who demands neither formal acquaintance nor definition. She cried out: 'My Lord, I have been oppressive to my soul. I surrender to the Lord of the worlds now with Sulayman." This *islām* is not our formal Islam. It is the real and 'essential' *islām*.

Again, the word 'muslim' is being used in the sense of *muslim* in the following verse: "And when Isa sensed disbelief from them, he asked, 'Who will be my helpers unto Allah?' The *hawāriyyūn* (disciples) said, 'We are the helpers of Allah; we believe in Allah; and bear witness (O Isa) that we are *muslim*s (submitting) to Allah." (3:52) The disciples of Isa are saying: 'we are *muslims*.' In all such verses, the words 'islām' and 'muslim' are being used in the 'essential' sense of *islām* and *muslim* respectively.

The following set of verses allude to the fact that surrender (*islām*) includes the component of surrendering to the communications of God in addition to surrendering to Him. The different communications of God are the same 'in essence'; they differ 'in form' due to being conveyed in differing circumstances:

He has ordained (sharaʿa) for you [O people] the same religion (dīn) that He enjoined upon Nuh, which We have revealed to you [Muhammad], and that which We enjoined upon Ibrahim and Musa and Isa: 'Uphold the religion (dīn) and do not divide [into factions] within it'. Dreadful for the polytheists is that which you [O Muhammad] call them to; Allah chooses for Himself whom He wills and guides to Himself whoever turns back [to Him]. (42:13)

It is the same religion being revealed time and again in accordance with the demands of the context (that is, the time, place, and people). Tweaks, changes, additions, and subtractions to the societal regulations of 'the one religion (*dīn*) of God' have occurred due to the different needs of differing contexts, giving rise to the different expressions of the same religion.

Consider the following verses:

When his (Ibrahim's) Lord said to him, 'Surrender.' He re-plied, 'I surrender [myself] to the Lord of the Universe.' And Ibrahim enjoined his sons with this, and [so did] Yaqub: 'My sons, indeed Allah has chosen for you the [true] religion (dīn); therefore, do not die save as muslimūn (those surrendered to Him or in a state of islām)." (2:131-2)

Here, the phrase "… Allah has chosen for you the [true] religion (*dīn*)…" refers to the 'formal' religion practiced by the children of Yaqub, consisting of dos and don'ts, and rights and wrongs, in accordance with the rational, moral, and spiritual demands of their context. The word 'muslimūn' refers to 'those surrendered to God and His communication (which is the formal religion)'. Thus, the word 'muslimūn' is being used here in the sense of *muslim*s, however it refers to 'those surrendered to God and His specific communication to them', which for the children of Yaqub was the formal organised religion they belonged to.

Therefore, the verse "Indeed, the *dīn* with Allah is *islām*" (3:19) refers to the state of surrender to God (*islām*) and to whatever He has communicated to the individual and the collectivity (which is, the 'formal' religion). Accordingly, the verse, "And whoever desires a religion (*dīn*) other than *islām*, it will never be accepted from him" (3:85), means that Allah does not accept the deeds of an individual who surrenders to other than Him and to other than His communication which was specifically meant for him and the collectivity he is a member of.

The following is a summary of the lecture thus far:

Firstly, the chronological reading of the verses of the Quran reveals that the term 'islām' does not refer to formal Islam (our religion) predominantly; rather, it refers to *islām*, which is the *essence* of formal Islam and all other monotheistic religions. Similarly, God uses the word 'muslim' in most verses to refer to the *muslim* and not the Muslim. In fact, the Quran is clear that the deeds of a Muslim subscribing to formal Islam will not be accepted so long as he is not internally surrendered to God (*muslim*). Hence, despite being Muslims and performing all the rituals of Islam, the adversaries of Imam Husayn are condemned due to their inner rejection of God.

Secondly, *islām* is the only 'religion (*dīn*) of Allah', and it has been delivered to the people of every prophet, that is, it has been conveyed time and again in differing contexts, hence the existence of the plurality of 'forms' or expressions. Every 'form' of the 'one religion (*dīn*) of Allah' has two components: one fixed and the other changing. The fixed component is 'to worship, serve, and surrender to Allah'. The changing component conveys the communication of what is pleasing to Allah in any given time and place, or in other words it pertains to what Allah deems is most effective in actualising our human godly potential in differing contexts.

Finally, all Christians, Jews, Zorostrians, Sabians, and Muslims are potentially *muslims* because all of them follow 'forms' of *islām* (which is 'the one religion (*dīn*) of Allah'). Allama Tabataba'i and others confirm that there has only ever been 'one *dīn* with Allah', and that there has not been any change in 'the *dīn* of Allah', for how can there be? How can the same God convey two or three different understandings of Himself? Obviously, He will convey the same understanding. If there is only One God, then His communication to humankind has to be one communication 'in essence'.

In this sense, the Quran is asserting that 'the one religion (*dīn*) of Allah' (*islām*) is *perennial*, that is, it has been the same reality and truth throughout history. It is the same God and the same message, and everyone has access to it. Thus, Allah says in the Quran that salvation is available to one and all, because it is possible for the adherents of all the different 'forms' of 'the one religion (*dīn*) of Allah' (or *islām*) to forge a meaningful relationship with God intuitively and attain salvation.

Consider the following verse in Sūra al-Ḥujurāt in which a significant number of Muslims are reprimanded for their attitude: "They consider they have obliged you [O Muhammad] by becoming Muslims. Say, 'Do not consider your Islam as a favour upon me, rather Allah has conferred a favour upon you [and has obliged you], inasmuch as He has guided you to the faith if you are truthful." (49:17) This was in response to Muslims entertaining the thought that they were doing Prophet Muhammad a favour by embracing his faith. Allah tells the Prophet to say: 'Do not oblige me with your formal Islam. Allah is doing you a favour insofar as He has guided you to the faith.' In other words, Allah is saying: 'Your mere acceptance of formal Islam does not mean much to Me in and of itself. I am not obliged to do anything because of it.'

A few verses before, Allah says: "The Bedouins say, 'we have deep-seated faith (*īmān*) [in Allah]'. Say [O Muhammad], 'You do not have deep-seated faith (*īmān*), but rather [you should] say [O Bedouins], 'we have embraced Islam', for deep-seated faith (*īmān*) has not yet entered within your hearts...'." (49:14) Before commenting on this verse, we need to note that the word 'muslim' was being used to refer to 'the members of Islam' (that is, the Muslims) by this point in the revelatory period, and not to 'those surrendered to God' (*muslims*); in other words, the change in the associated meaning of the word 'muslim' had occurred in the minds of the people by this time.

In this verse, Allah uses the verb *aslamnā* (which is the first-person plural of the verbal form of the word "muslim") to signify 'we have accepted uppercase Islam', and He uses the verbal derivatives of word *īmān* to mean 'deep-seated faith'. The verse conveys that those Bedouin Muslims had not attained 'deep-seated faith' in their hearts; rather, they had merely embraced Islam. This means the two are not the same: a person can be a Muslim nominally and yet not have 'deep-seated faith' in the heart. Allah considers the mere acceptance of Islam as a totally different species of commitment in comparison to 'deep-seated faith' (*īmān*) and belonging to Him. Accordingly, He corrects the self-deception of the individuals referred to in this verse who thought that the mere acceptance of Islam is equivalent to 'deep-seated faith' (*īmān*).

Let us discuss the component of 'surrendering to the communication of God', which is the second component of 'surrender' in *islām* (the first being 'surrendering to God'). The communication of God has changed over time in accordance with differing rational, moral, and spiritual demands of different peoples in different times and places. This explains why Prophet Muhammad abrogated certain parts of the mosaic law and kept other parts (that continue to be part of our Sharia today). For instance, the Quran states, "We prescribed for them therein (Torah): the life for the life, and the eye for the eye, and the nose for the nose, and the ear for the ear, and the tooth for the tooth..." (5:45). This regulation is still part of the Sharia of Islam. Therefore, a lot of the regulations formulated for Prophet Musa's society were relevant for Prophet Muhammad's community, but many others were abrogated because the demands of the individual and collectivity had changed.

Coming back to the second component of *islām*, since a considerable number of the dos and don'ts in the divine communication have changed over time, it follows that some formulations pertaining to the same issue will be more accurate and up to date than others (and often, they will be the latest ones).

We can debate which of them is the most appropriate, but the fact that Allah says, "Say [O Muhammad], O People of the Book, you are upon nothing until you establish the Torah and the Gospel." (5:68), affirms the efficacy of the previous 'forms' of the devotional and societal regulations of these other religions. The natural conclusion of the notion of change in the dos and don'ts in the divine communication together with God affirming the efficacy of previous formulations, is *religious and legal pluralism.*

Consider the following verse again: "This day, I have completed your religion (*dīn*) for you…" (5:3) Allah is being very particular when He states, "… *your dīn* for you…". In effect, He is saying: 'It is a tailor-made version of *islām* for you, O Muslims. I have completed it in accordance with the demands of *your* society.' There is a big difference between God informing the seventh century Arabian community (or even just the Arabian community for that matter) of the completion of their *dīn* (or their 'form' of *islām*), and Him addressing the entirety of the global Muslim community for all of time and space and informing them of the completion of their *dīn* (or their 'form' of *islām*). The changing component of the *dīn* will of necessity be different in different contexts.

It is an accepted fact that the regulations of 'the *dīn* of Allah' have been abrogated several times in the period between the prophethoods of Prophets Musa and Muhammad due to the differing needs and demands of the community. Hence, regulations were added, deleted, and modified in light of the 'essence' of the *dīn* (which is "surrendering to Allah") to optimise the efficacy of regulations. It is absurd to insist that the context, needs, and demands of the people have not altered in the last fourteen hundred years. The human collectivity has grown exponentially in the period after the death of Prophet Muhammad in comparison to its growth prior to it. Thus, if changes during the period between the prophethoods of Prophets Musa and Muhammad resulted in God sending several messages refashioning the 'formal' component of 'the *dīn* of Allah' in light of its 'essence', then is it reasonable to assert that the 'formal' component can never change after the death of Prophet Muhammad despite humankind growing constantly due to the existential feature of incessant evolutionary motion? Obviously not.

To reiterate, when scholars cite the verse, "This day, I have completed your religion (*dīn*) for you..." (5:3), it is understood naïvely to signify that everything pertaining to Islam has been conveyed, and hence there cannot be any change. By asserting this, are we saying that human beings were constantly changing and evolving in the period between the prophethoods of Musa and Muhammad but that after Prophet Muhammad, humankind has stopped moving, growing, changing, and evolving? Human beings have experienced more change in the last two hundred years than in all their previous history combined. Today's notion of human rights, and its global approval, did not exist prior to the formation of the United Nations. (Of course, that is not to say that the blessed Prophet Muhammad did not initiate the trend of human rights in his own context.)

Now if we accept the assertion of scholars that everything pertaining to Islam has been conveyed at the time of the Prophet, then are we prepared to be indifferent to the possession of slaves, having 'right-hand' possessions, beating wives, and marrying infants? Are we saying that all such regulations of Islam are divine and so must be retained the way they are? Should we take *jizya* (the tax for non-Muslims) from the Jews and Christians, and make everyone who does not belong to the Abrahamic faiths stateless? Is this what the modern Muslim believes and wants? Such issues are the implications of what the majority of Muslims believe: that Islam is the only true and righteous religion, and that it is the complete religion of Allah for all of humankind. Both beliefs are mere assumptions that need to be checked very critically.

Think about it carefully: *islām* is a salient flowing reality; it is fluid, and it flows. It has one stable component which is salvific, and that is 'to tend to Allah genuinely'. The other component pertains to *how* one is to attain the good pleasure of God in a particular context; hence, this component can never be stable and must change of necessity. Now if this component has undergone changes in the past, then what has made it become stable and immutable now and today?

It is true that 'the one *dīn* of Allah' is the only acceptable *dīn* for humankind. However, this means it always has to be in sync with the human condition. Now the human condition is one of fluidity and evolution, hence 'the one *dīn* of Allah' has to be fluid and evolve as well. Thus, societal regulations facilitating a virtuous and moral life for the individuals of a collectivity have to be re-evaluated constantly within the dynamic and evolutionary human context. The stable component of 'the one *dīn* of Allah' is God-centricity, but *how* to become godly is always subject to change and fluctuation; in other words, the devotional and societal regulations can be modified so that they remain optimal in facilitating growth of the individual and collectivity.

Narrations state that the Muslims will contend with the Twelfth Imam: 'This is not the *dīn* of Prophet Muhammad; you have brought something else.' It stands to reason that his grandfather's *dīn* had to change in accordance with the needs and demands of society. I am not implying or advocating in any way that we do away with prayers, fasting, and so on. On the contrary, these are the permanent practices of devotion; they strengthen the attitude of God-centricity in the mind of the Muslim individual and give the sense of a religious identity to the collectivity; in any case, they are very few in number. The vast majority of what comprises Islam is its huge body of regulations on all the various types of human interaction, system of rights, and so on. These societal regulations comprise the majority of Islam as a 'form' of 'the *dīn* of Allah', and they are always subject to change.

Lecture Four
Spiritual Morlaity and No-Finality of Sharias

The word *islām* was used by the Prophet Ibrahim to refer to 'the state of surrender to Allah' alone (and no other deities). We can extrapolate this from the following verses of the Quran: "And strive hard in [the way of] Allah, [such] a striving as is due to Him; He has chosen you and has not laid upon you a hardship in religion; the archetypical religion (*milla*) of your father Ibrahim; He named you *muslims* before and in this [revelation]…" (22:78) and

> *Ibrahim was not a Jew nor a Christian, but he was a ḥanīf, a muslim (one surrendered to God), and he was not of the polytheists. Indeed, those of humankind who have the best claim to Ibrahim are those who followed him, and this Prophet and those who believe; and Allah is the Protector of the believers. (3:67–8)*

Similarly, the verses of Sūra al-Kāfirūn, "Say [O Muhammad], 'O disbelievers, I do not worship what you worship'" (109:1-2), emphasise that the 'essence' of 'the one *dīn* of Allah' (or the 'essence' of *islām*, which is surrendering to God and His communication) is to tend to the One God and to surrender to His authority as opposed to the authority of other deities and idols.

This feature of *islām* is the 'essence' of all monotheistic faiths. Hence, the Quran exhorts the People of the Book to establish a memorandum of the commonality between themselves on the basis of devotion to the One God alone:

Say, 'O People of the Book, let us come to a position that is common between us and you, that we serve none but God, and that we do not associate anything with Him, and that none of us takes others as lords beside God.' And if they turn their backs [from you O Muhammad and believers], say: 'Bear witness that we are muslims.' (3:64)

This verse affirms what we discussed in the previous lecture that devotion to the One God is the 'essence' of all monotheistic religions, and hence they are all different 'forms' of *islām*. We also discussed how the word 'muslim' is used predominantly by Allah in the sense of *muslim*, referring to 'one who surrenders to the authority of God'. In addition to the proclamation of the One God, monotheistic faiths share another fundamental feature: the necessity of attaining a virtuous state, for it is both the means and end of surrendering to God. God-conscious behaviour, stemming from such a virtuous and godly state, is at the heart of the repetition of the verses in Sūra al-Kāfirūn: "Say [O Muhammad], 'O disbelievers, I do not worship what you worship, and you are not worshipping what I worship, nor am I worshipping what you have worshipped, neither are you worshipping what I worship, for you is your religion (*dīn*), and for me is my religion (*dīn*)." (109:1-6)

According to the Quran, the polytheists of Mecca believed in Allah as either the highest God Who was the cause of all the other gods, or the only real God Who could be worshipped by means of idol-worship (see 29:61, 43:87, 10:18, and 39:3). Thus, the Meccans were worshiping Allah in one way or another. Why then are they termed 'disbelievers'?

Consider the following verse from Sūra al-Bayyina: "Those who disbelieved among the People of the Book and the polytheists could not have desisted (erring) till the clear proof came unto them." (98:1) Here the disbelief (*kufr*) of some of the People of the Book does not mean disbelief in the One God obviously; it refers to their rejection of the communication of God. This reasoning applies to the polytheists as well by virtue of the verse mentioning them alongside the People of the Book. Therefore, *islām* does not merely equate to a proclamation of a belief in God but includes accepting and living in accordance with His communication, which 'in essence' is to exert oneself continually and consciously to acquire a virtuous godly state. Hence, the Quran rebukes the polytheists for claiming that their inhumane and unchaste practices were ordained by Allah: "And when they commit an indecent act, they say, 'we found our fathers doing it and Allah enjoined it upon us.' Say, 'Allah does not ordain indecency…'" (7:28)

Therefore, an indispensable part of God-centricity is acknowledging that God is the Most Perfect in His morals and is the Principle of all goodness. We are required to aspire to become like Him and attain godliness by having faith in Him. Every faith professing belief in the One God that I have come across, advocates the existence of a supremely moral and virtuous God, and defines the goal of humankind as 'the actualisation of humanity in His beautiful image'.

Within the domain of religion then, morality is not merely committing the right act because it is the right thing to do, rather it is to perform the right act for the sake of God's pleasure and the attainment of godliness. Cultivation of this attitude with respects to one's actions constitutes part of 'surrendering to God', and it gradually results in the emergence of godliness and the actualisation of the human potential. Accordingly, we term it as 'spiritual morality'. A fuller discussion on spiritual morality will be conducted in forthcoming lecture series, however due to its relevance at present, we will discuss it to the extent needed.

Morality is a highly analytical discipline today. It has developed from the ancient Greek philosophers' attempts to define 'the good life' and how we ought to lead 'a good life'. Morality today addresses all issues pertaining to voluntary human action. According to me, a moral or good action is determined in light of the existential principle (or property) of growth. In other words, the right action is the one that is most productive in all three aspects of the individual and collectivity: the rational, moral, and spiritual. Hence, speaking the truth, keeping trust, being charitable, and giving life are morally good actions because they are productive in all the three aspects of the being of the individual and collectivity. The existential principle (or property) of growth also informs us that concealing the truth is moral in situations in which revealing the truth compromises the life and safety of oneself or others.

The rights of others are determined in different contexts by the application of 'the principle of justice' and will differ from context to context. This is because the appreciation (or understanding) of 'the principle of justice' depends on the degree of growth of 'human nobility' (which is the innate sense of compassion, decency, and godliness within humankind) of the collectivity in any given time and place; hence, the appreciation of 'the principle of justice' will vary in different collectivities and as a result, so will the rights of others. Justice is to give everything its rightful due; however, since our 'existential aptitudes' (which refers to the psychological, cognitive, and moral aptitudes of human beings) are becoming gradually more refined due to the evolutionary nature of existence (or in other words, due to its property of growth), and since the status of the 'just' action is unstable, defining 'what the *just* action is' will need constant evaluation and possible tweaking. Similarly, the constant refinement of 'human nobility' (again due to the existential property of growth) will give humans a greater sense of dignity, compassion, and decency, which will refine their appreciation of the 'just' and moral act. Examples of this include the abolishment of slavery and the abhorrence towards child labour felt by most of humankind today.

The acquisition of virtues or 'spiritual morality' is the means to becoming godly. It is personal and subjective; in other words, virtues are acquired by means of our subjective or inner interactions prior to, during, and after the performance of both devotional and non-devotional acts. Hence, an act performed sincerely with the intention of seeking proximity to God is expected to contribute to the actualisation of godliness, God willing. The ideal of godliness or 'being godly' by means of acquiring virtues and behaving morally, is common to all faiths irrespective of whether they advocate a narrower sense of monotheism or otherwise. The Quran uses the word 'muslim' in the sense of the *muslim* to describe the state of previous prophets and their followers, for they had surrendered to God and acquired the virtuous state by behaving morally and surrendering to God Who is the Principle of all virtues.

In addition to 'spiritual morality', God has prescribed specific devotions for the people of each faith by means of which they can surrender to Him. These constitute the 'forms' of behaviour, which the Quran terms as *sharia*. The word *sharia* can be used to signify the communication of God in its totality, meaning both its theology and regulations, however we will be employing it in its common usage signifying 'regulations' only. Generally, regulations can be divided into 'devotional' and 'societal'. Sharia regulations are not stable 'forms', just like the 'just' action; they are subject to a constant state of flux. We will discuss 'the existential state of flux' in the next lecture. Consider the following verse:

> *He has ordained (shara'a) for you [O people] the same religion (dīn) that He enjoined upon Nuh, which We have revealed to you [Muhammad], and that which We enjoined upon Ibrahim and Musa and Isa: 'Uphold the religion (dīn) and do not divide [into factions] within it'... (42:13)*

Thus, Isa, Musa, Ibrahim, Nuh, and other prophets were given their respective *sharias*. Recall: every *sharia* is part of the second component of 'the one *dīn* of Allah' (or *islām*), which is 'surrendering to the communication of God'; 'the communication of God' is contingent upon the context (that is, the time, place, and people); and the context is subject to flux because the nature of existence is continual change and motion. Therefore, every *sharia* is subject to flux and hence in need of constant scrutiny and periodic revision so that its potential in facilitating growth towards God is kept optimal. The implication here is that there is no sacredness to the 'form' of the regulation in and of itself. Sacredness is ascribable to the 'essence' of the regulation alone. Consider the following verse:

> *Say [O believers], 'We [Muslims] believe in Allah and what has been revealed to us and what was revealed to Ibrahim, Ismail, Ishaq, Yaqub, and the Tribes, and [we believe in] what was given to Musa and Isa, and what was given to the prophets from their Lord; we do not make any distinction between any of them (the prophets), and we surrender to Him. (2:136)*

We know the *sharia* of each prophet was different, so what is the meaning of "we [the Muslims] believe in... what was revealed to Ibrahim, Ismail, Ishaq, Yaqub and the Tribes, and what was given to Musa and Isa, and what was given to the prophets... We do not differentiate between any of them"? How is it possible to believe in all the different *sharias*, for that would require us to believe in many contradictory and contrary regulations? Therefore, the verse can only mean 'we [the Muslims] believe in... the *essence* of whatever has been revealed to Ibrahim, Ismail, Ishaq, Yaqub and the Tribes, and *the essence* of whatever was given to Musa and Isa, and *the essence* of whatever was given to the prophets... [and] hence we do not differentiate between any of them [because *in essence* they are the same]'.

Recall that the nature of a 'form' is to differ and be different to every other 'form', for instance the 'forms' of humans differ from one another by virtue of their 'forms'. Similarly, the 'forms' of regulations differ also, resulting in the phenomenon of multiple *sharias* (or regulatory systems), which is mentioned in the Quran: "We have assigned a law and a path to each [group of people]… So compete [with each other] in good deeds (*khayrāt*)." (5:48) For 'deeds' to qualify as 'good', their performance must be accompanied by the first and second components of 'the one *dīn* of Allah' (or *islām*), which is 'surrendering to God' and 'surrendering to His communication' respectively. In other words, the performance of such a deed must be firstly accompanied with the intention of seeking proximity to God and secondly compliant with the 'forms' of the regulations of the *sharia* of the performer.

Before continuing, a couple of points need elaboration:

Firstly, the fact that there are multiple *sharias* according to the Quran means there is no centrality to any one *sharia*. If there was centrality to just one *sharia*, meaning that if only one *sharia* had to be followed because it was the only salvific and hence correct one, then Allah would have mentioned and singled it out, for He binds Himself to speak the truth. Similarly, He would have informed us that only the adherents of that particular *sharia* are going to evolve into godliness, and nobody else; in other words, He would have made it clear that the members of one religion only – that is, either the Jews, Christians, Hindus, Buddhists, or Muslims – have the potential for salvation, and nobody else. However, in contrast to this Allah promises salvation to all who surrender to Him via their own respective 'formal' *sharias*.

Secondly, when a person performs the *ṣalāt* with presence of mind and heart, and becomes mindful of God, then the interaction (the presence of mind and heart) and action (the *ṣalāt*) together constitute 'the righteous deed'. Therefore, if a Jew performs the Jewish 'form' of *ṣalāt* with presence of mind and heart, and becomes mindful of God, then such action and interaction constitute 'the righteous deed'. This also applies to the Christian, Hindu, Sabian, and whoever else is monotheistic: if they perform their respective 'forms' of devotions with presence of mind and heart, and become mindful of God, then such action and interaction constitute 'the righteous deed'. Such action and interaction in the domain of devotional acts result in the flourishing of godliness within the human soul.

This brings us to the next question: Does salvation depend upon believing in and following one prophet only and no others? Must there be the centrality in the domain of devotion, instruction, and guidance to just one prophet, for instance to Prophet Muhammad, and nobody else? Take any two prophets. Tell me which of them states, 'Lying is good', 'Cheating is good', 'Do not be centred towards God'? Has any prophet said such things? Obviously not. They have all conveyed the same message of God as far as morality and spirituality are concerned. All prophets have said the same thing; they have all conveyed the same message. It is the same message being delivered time and again.

You may then enquire: If the messages of the different prophets are all the same, then how are they different? They are different with respect to the specific devotional and societal regulations instituted by each prophet on *how* to be spiritual and moral human beings. The regulations of each prophet were formulated in accordance with the needs and demands of the context. This is the only difference; otherwise, they are the same 'in essence'. They all say the same thing with regard to spirituality and universal moral maxims. As we grew, progressed, and became increasingly sophisticated during the course of human history, prophets were sent to remind us of what the previous prophets had said, and if necessary, they fashioned the same truths differently (by modifying, adding, or deleting devotional and societal regulations in accordance with the context). What has always been of paramount importance is the preservation of those *truths*, as opposed to 'the *forms*' (or expressions) of those *truths* per se.

This is very important to retain, so I am going to repeat it once more:

Observe the person who believes that Ram and Krishna were godly and saintly men. Does he believe this because Ram and Krishna were cheats, liars, cowards, thieves, and murderers? No, he venerates Ram and Krishna because they were godly, truthful, brave, generous, and forgiving. Do the people who venerate Isa, venerate him because he was a cheat, liar, coward, thief, and murderer? No. You begin to see that it is the same truth with different faces and labels. It the same truth. We are required to realise and embody the same truth that these grand people were. Our salvation and success do not lie in merely stating and believing, 'I follow this prophet and that religion.' Our success lies in *becoming* godly people like these prophets. If you become like the blessed Prophet, then you have become Isa, Musa, Ram, and Buddha, all of them all at once, and that is your success. Accordingly, the Quran has removed centrality from the prophets. It exhorts us to tend to Allah and nobody else.

The root of the *exclusivism* of the Muslims, Christians, Jews, and Hindus is that each organised religion or faith attributes the 'essence' of religion to their respective founders and their teachings. This has resulted in the demonising, vilifying, and killing of the 'other' because the 'other' is viewed as wrong and hence inferior. However, prophets, saints, and godly souls as means of conveying the truth were never supposed to be central to the message. By giving them centrality, the faithful of each organised religion, faith, or sect have been able to point fingers at each other. We need to rectify our thinking. Just as we say in the United Nations that there are certain inalienable human rights (or common human values) that all humans have and share by virtue of being human, irrespective of whether one is black, white, brown, rich, poor, young, or old; similarly, we need to recognise that there is a spirituality – by which I mean a consciousness, religion, and an understanding – that embraces humankind at large. However, we need more material to assist us in seeing the truth of this.

I agree that the theology and religious practices of some religions may have been misinterpreted or even perverted, however the sincere faithful of those religions believe them to be true, and they are 'certain' of their accuracy. Here we resort to 'the principle of certitude' (that our scholars discuss and utilise in the Islamic sciences) to substantiate intellectual religious diversity. If somebody is 'certain' of something, then they cannot be expected to not act in accordance with their 'certainty' and to not be affected and influenced by it; on the contrary, they are excused for acting in accordance with their 'certainty' if it is mistaken, and they cannot be held to account and punished for not behaving contrary to their 'certainty'. For instance, if a person is delusional but 'certain' that there is a giant scorpion here, then he will be affected by that 'certainty' and behave accordingly. He will not be blamed for screaming, shouting, and running away, rather he will be excused, because 'certainty' either compels or obliges one to act in accordance with it. Thus, one cannot expect an individual's 'certainty' to not be impactful on their attitude and behaviour.

Similarly, if someone is 'certain' that Isa was the final prophet, then you cannot condemn him for holding that view and acting in accordance with it, because 'certainty' either compels or obliges the individual to adopt that view and to behave according to it; hence the individual is excused for adopting that view and behaving according to it, and he cannot be held to account or punished for holding it. Now, if somebody is 'certain' the earth is flat, then they cannot be expected to not act in accordance with this 'certainty' and to not be affected and influenced by it; hence they will interpret the rest of the universe in accordance with their 'certainty' of the flatness of earth. Now despite being excused and not accountable or punishable for believing in this, we are permitted to discuss the basis of their 'certainty' and try to convince them otherwise. For instance, we might say: 'If the earth is flat, then why does it appear as a beautiful globe when we look at the earth via satellites'. Therefore, we are free to try to undermine the basis of the 'certainty', however we cannot expect 'certainty' to not compel or oblige the individual to adopt a particular view and behaviour, and we cannot expect them to not be affected and influenced by it. This is what the Quran exhorts: 'Debate with the People of the Book in the most beautiful manner, but do not condemn them or say that they do not have salvation, for I (Allah) have given them salvation.'

> *[O Believers], do not argue with the People of the Book save in the best manner, except those of them that do wrong; and say, 'We believe in what was revealed to us and in what was revealed to you; our God and your God are one [and the same], and to Him we have surrendered.' (29:46)*

A Muslim may have a more accurate understanding but that does not mean the sincere non-Muslim believer cannot be honoured for their sincerity and devotion to God based on their own understanding. Similarly, it also does not mean that we should not engage with other sincere religious believers to learn from each other and rectify each other's minds. This is definitely allowed insofar as one engages in the most beautiful way. Ultimately, they have found God and worship Him in a different manner and perhaps with a less refined understanding, but they know what godliness means intuitively, and hence they are growing towards godliness.

It is like pointing out to a university student that their textbook is outdated, but they insist they are 'certain' they have the best book. You cannot blame the university student for insisting on this because the 'certainty' compels them to adopt the view that it is the best book and obliges them to behave according to it (their 'certainty'). Thus, one cannot expect the student to not be affected and influenced by their 'certainty'. One cannot expect the university student to abandon reading the old edition of the textbook as long as their 'certainty' regarding the old edition remains. However, one can question and try to reason with them. For instance, one may ask the student: 'When was it printed?' After having been informed that it was printed few years ago, one can ask the following question: 'Has the scientific world progressed in the interim or not?' At this point, the student may begin to realise and say: 'Yes, it has. I need to get the later edition of the textbook because it will have those scientific discoveries that are not in the previous edition.' We should discuss with the student in this way. However, it would be wrong of us to tell the student: 'You will fail the exam if you don't have the latest edition of the textbook.' This is because the previous edition is adequate for passing the exam, which is to get forty five percent. In fact, it is possible for the student to get eighty per cent or more, without having learnt the new discoveries made in the interim period.

I hope the issue is a bit clearer. We appreciate people when we understand them in their own contexts. The Quran appreciates people, communities, nations, and religions in exactly the same way. We are also duty bound to share the beautiful truth Allah has given us, but only if the opportunity presents itself, and not in an arrogant way, and certainly not with the view to convert anybody. The Quran states that in truth only Allah guides and nobody else. The blessed Prophet used to get frustrated due to the slow uptake of his message in Mecca. He could not understand why the people were unable to accept such a lucid and rational message. Allah would say to him: 'It is not your job to convert anybody. Just convey the message in the best possible manner. Leave the rest to Me.' (See 28:56 and 88:21-22)

Now we will discuss Islam (our religion), and the claim of the Muslims that it is the best communication because it is the latest edition. Do you have hearts broad enough to listen to what I am going to say? Based on the trend expressed in the Quran of reformulating the *sharia* in accordance with changes in the context, our edition has been outdated for quite a while and is in dire need of updating. We Muslims are so complacent; we proudly assert: 'We have the best version!' Yes, it was the best version of societal regulations for the context in which those regulations were formulated. When the context changes, it is no longer 'the best version'.

I know what you are thinking: 'Is he going to say, "there is a new revelation"'? No, there is not; be assured, there is not. Prophet Muhammad was the final prophet, and those societal regulations were ordained as part of the final revelation in a formalistic sense. However, the Quran states the same religion is being delivered since the time of Prophet Nuh. Each later communication differs from earlier ones in terms of the 'forms' (like societal regulations) while retaining the 'essence' (which is God-centricity). This presupposes a perpetually evolving human community and continually changing circumstances. Now since the human community and circumstances have continued to evolve and change, how is it conceivable that societal regulations governing human societal interactions of seventh century Muslim Arabia are immutable and remain applicable for all of time?

Recall, it is the 'essence' of monotheistic religions that is eternal, immutable, and universal. The 'essence' is to surrender to God in the most beautiful way, which means giving ourselves over to God lovingly, so that He may nurture us and bring us of age. At this point, the soul of the individual returns to the Lord of the Spirit, and He begins to manifest Himself beautifully within the individual. "Return to your Lord, well-pleased [with Him], well-pleasing [to Him]." (89:28) This 'returning to God' and 'reflecting the beauty of God' is the 'essence' of every monotheistic religion.

The fluctuating factor is *how* to surrender to God. This is because '*how* to surrender to God' will differ according to the demands and needs of the context. Here, there is 'no finality'. If there was 'finality', there would not have been any changes in the communications to Nuh, Ibrahim, Musa, Isa, and the blessed Prophet. However, all the communications of God were different and yet the same. Their 'forms' were different, and yet their 'essence' was the same. The '*how* to' was different, and yet the 'surrender' was the same. The fact that the *sharia* of each prophet was a different 'form' of the same moral and spiritual truths, specifically tailored to the needs and demands of a particular context, demonstrates there is 'no finality' in the 'formal' aspects of religion, and that stands to reason.

The human condition is one of constant evolution. The language, method, reasoning, and examples used to express moral truths to children are inappropriate when expressing the same truths to adults. For instance, the communication of the duty of being truthful and righteous will be formulated differently when addressing adults. It is the same truth, but it is being refashioned. Allama Tabataba'i has a beautiful discussion on the meaning of *al-ṣirāt al-mustaqīm* (as in when we say *Ihdinā al-ṣirat al-mustaqīm* – "guide us to the right path" – 1:6). He says that *al-ṣirāt al-mustaqīm* (the right path) is not one path; rather, it consists of all the paths or stages of one's life. This means *al-ṣirāt al-mustaqīm* includes all the different conceptions of the same spirituality we held throughout our lives as we evolved and grew. For instance, we prayed *du'ā* at the age of sixteen because we wanted to pass an exam. Then we prayed it at the age of twenty because we desired the Layla of our dreams. At the age of twenty-two, we made it because we wanted children. At the age of twenty-five, we prayed it because we needed sustenance. We made it at the age of forty because we did not want to die young, and so on at the ages of fifty, sixty, and seventy. At some point, we pray *du'ā* because we want our Lord, and so we exclaim "*Ya Rabbī!*". The intensity is so great that the Throne (*'arsh*) begins to tremble with us. The angels begin to sing with us. The same God has been called upon from the age of sixteen till the age of sixty. It is the same God but our relationship with Him has fluctuated and changed altogether. So, *al-ṣirāt al-mustaqīm* is not one path. It comprises different paths coming together to construct one path of evolutionary growth and self-realisation into godliness.

Humankind is continually growing. Would you say that the societal norms and regulations appropriate for the time of the Prophets Musa and Isa are valid today? Your answer will be 'no' obviously. Well, how about those formulated for the time of Prophet Muhammad? Are they valid today? Today we have the notion of human rights due to a more sophisticated societal set up. Is it right to take slaves today? Obviously not, and yet the Quran condones slavery. Is it right to have 'right-hand' possessions? Is it right to ask an astrophysicist to bring another woman with her when bearing testimony? Obviously not. Even though such norms and regulations are in the Quran, your intuition cannot accept them as valid today, for they do not make sense. Is it right to beat one's wife? Obviously not. Your intuition knows this is absolutely unacceptable today, and yet it is in the Quran. Clearly, no societal 'form' can be 'final' or absolute due to our evolutionary nature.

The Sharia needs to be a guidance for the evolving human community. Accordingly, it must be fashioned and refashioned expressing those salient beautiful moral truths appropriately in and for different eras, locales, and degrees of human evolution and growth, as was the case prior to and during the lifetime of the blessed Prophet. Is it wrong to have Christian and Jewish friends? Obviously not, and yet some will quote the Quran: "O you who believe, do not take the Jews and Christians as allies; they are allies [only] to each other." (5:51)

In conclusion, the second component of *islām*, which pertains to the issue of '*how to* surrender to God', is in a constant state of flux. This means it has to change periodically to continue to be optimal in assisting the rational, moral, and spiritual growth of its adherents. The first component of *islām* is eternal, immutable, and universal; it is to surrender to God and become godlike, which means tending to Him alone as opposed to other than

Him, and finding Him intuitively through our human condition. We will explain in the next lecture why the second component is 'right' for a particular space and time and hence is stable for that time, and how it is wrong for other contexts. I would like to end with the following examples:

Today, the practice of having servants is acceptable, is it not? In the future, it will be viewed as the greatest crime because 'human nobility' – the innate sense of dignity, compassion, decency, and godliness within humankind – at that point will not allow for the servitude of one human to another. Today, eating meat is a practice accepted by society; however, when we are able to communicate with animals in the future, it may become unacceptable, for it will be very difficult to tell a lamb: 'I am going to eat you tonight.' My nobility will not allow it. Thus, we may not be eating meat in a future world, for it may be regarded as unacceptable even though it is acceptable today. In a thousand years' time, we hope humankind will not deem us as barbarians for eating meat. Similarly, we hope they will not view us as unjust for having servants, for it is 'just' in this context, and hence we do not even see its wrongfulness. By the time of the revelation of the Quran, the practice of stoning people to death was deemed to be wrong, but in Mosaic law it was regarded as an acceptable 'form' of punishment. The second component of religion is always on the move.

Lecture Five
Flux and Mutability of the Quranic Regulations

Islam has two components, just like any other 'form' of *islām*: the first is the salient 'essence', which is becoming God-centric and acquiring the virtuous state, and the second is the means to attain the 'essence'. These means consist of devotional and societal regulations. Devotional regulations differ from one faith to another, and societal regulations are always in a state of flux. Here, a question may arise: If the Quran itself states that 'the *dīn*' is 'Islam' and it is 'complete' (as in the verse, "This day, I have completed *your* religion (*dīn*) for *you*…" (5:3)), then who are we to challenge it? This is a rational question. The Quran is no ordinary Book. It is the final communication from God. If the Quran states something as clearly and unambiguously as this verse, then how can anyone contend that the Quran does not mean what it is saying in its literal capacity? This is a challenging question and requires a befitting response.

Let us consider the actions of ISIS, and their likes, who use verses of the Quran to justify their atrocious behaviours. We normally disassociate with such extremist actions. However, ISIS argue that whatever they do is clearly and unambiguously stated in the Quran. None can deny that the practices of 'taking slaves' and 'killing the enemy of God' are stated in the Quran. This fact coupled with our belief in the 'divinity' and 'finality' of the Word of God force us to concede to the validity of their actions despite it not feeling right to us. So, on the one hand we are forced to believe in the truth of what they are doing, and on the other hand our intuition tells us that their actions are abhorrent. Our embarrassment in front of the human community forces us to say hypocritically that the Quran does not mean what it says, and yet on the basis of our theological assumptions and beliefs about the Quran, we have to concede that in reality we either believe secretly that the Quran means exactly what it says, or we are forced to believe that it does.

The initial audience of the revelation was appealed towards its rationality. The verses challenged the norms, practices, and status quo of the time. They shed light upon the irrational nature of Meccan devotional and societal regulations. The Quran is replete with verses exhorting us to think, reflect, and reason. This was the great appeal of Islam: it appealed to human reason making it the benchmark by which people could repudiate their formerly held beliefs and verify the content of revelation. It was a liberating experience. Indeed, the Quran refers to this liberation in the following verse: "…. He [Muhammad] enjoins them 'the good' and prohibits them 'the reprehensible'. He makes lawful to them the wholesome things and makes unlawful to them the unwholesome things; he relieves them of their burdens and the shackles which were upon them." (7:157)

The question arising here is: How were some members of the audience able to assent *immediately* to the accuracy of the verses of the Quran upon hearing them, for human reason requires time to examine, verify, and justify the content of any speech? In other words, since the realisation of the truth of the Quran was instantaneous for some of the audience and hence too quick for human reason to examine all perspectives, verify, and then justify them, how were they able to affirm the truth of the verses as they were hearing them? What was the mechanism by which they were able know the truth of the verses as they were being conveyed in real time?

The verses and injunctions of the Quran appealed to such members of its audience *intuitively* in their existential capacity. Our existential state or the nature of our existence is one of growth. This means intuition can know immediately that a particular norm or regulation is growth-promoting, just, and noble, and hence has moral value, after which human reason affirms the intuitive knowledge having only partially seen the justifications for that particular norm or regulation. Thus, the faculties of intuition and reason in many souls were able to assent instantly to the message of God-centricity and the truth and efficacy of the societal regulations upon hearing the revelation.

If the Quran was being revealed today with verses like those the extremists adhere to, would they appeal to anyone's faculty of intuition or reason? If the Prophet was here today, and if he issued verses instructing that women should receive half the share of inheritance of men in a societal setup in which women are both carers and providers, would that appeal to anyone's innate sense of justice and 'human nobility'? Today if the Prophet used phrases such as 'Beat your women…', 'Take slaves', 'Flog people in public', or 'Take right-hand possessions', would we not contend that these are inconsistent with 'human nobility' and dignity? Would such regulations appeal to the masses? Would they assent and proclaim that it is from God, the All-Mighty? I am asking you these questions genuinely. If you and I were not Muslims, and we were faced with a religion that had such commandments and phrases, would we give it a second thought? Would we call these regulations progressive and liberating, or would we say they are regressive, discriminatory, and uncivilised? This is a simple question, and yet we are so frightened to answer. We dare not say 'no', and we dare not accept either. We are in a state of limbo, are we not?

Look at our situation: On the one hand, the Quran is the Word of God, and so we cannot answer the above questions honestly, for that would be tantamount to opposing and rejecting the Quran. On the other hand, we believe nobody else should entertain and discuss such questions and verses either, because that entails blasphemy. It is a simple equation and calculation in our minds, is it not? To answer the above questions honestly is to deny the Word of God, which is tantamount to the denial of the authority of God and hence blasphemy, and we are frightened of committing an act of blasphemy. To do so would be *kufr*, and hence we would be procuring the fire and Hell. It is a simple calculation in our minds.

This same reasoning is undertaken by the Hindu. He has the same equation and calculation in his mind regarding his holy scriptures, and so he prefers to remain silent too. The result is the perpetuation of the unjust caste system. Similarly, the Christian makes the same calculation regarding trinitarian theology and remains committed to it despite it not making sense logically. The same is the case with the Jew. He has the same equation in his mind and makes the same calculation. He chooses to remain silent regarding the belief of the superiority of Jews over gentiles (non-Jews). Hence, he becomes indifferent to the plight of the rest of the people of the world. Thus, the rights of the gentiles, which includes treating them and their property with due respect, can be encroached upon at will. Look at the crises in the modern world and how the naïve assumptions we hold about our religious scriptures have contributed to it.

Those who first heard the Quran being recited, and who later became the Sahaba, were not like us who take birth into the faith. They were not beholden to the faith, and so they had a free reign and would often say unhesitatingly: 'O Muhammad, this does not make sense to us. Please explain it. If it makes sense after that, we will accept it, but if it does not, we will reject it, for we are not beholden to your God or your message until we commit to it;

however, we will only commit to it if it makes sense to us.' Is this not the attitude of a human being in a state of 'neutrality'? This point of 'neutrality' quickly disappears when we are born within organised faiths and religions, because the indoctrination of *exclusivism* and the inferiority of everything and everyone 'other' is part of every 'formal' religious worldview, culture, schooling, and public lecturing (*majālis*). The result is a delusional state: The members of every organised faith and religion live with a false sense of security.

Does the Quran not condemn the pagans for their uncritical adherence to the cultures of their forefathers? Consider the following verse: "… They [the disbelievers] say, 'rather, we follow what we found our forefathers following.' What! Even though their forefathers did not understand anything…?" (2:170) In fact, Allah expects us to critically evaluate the Quran and its content: "Will they not ponder on the Quran? If it had been from other than Allah, they would have found much inconsistency therein." (4:82).

Today, if most Muslims are asked whether there are any discrepancies within the Quran, they will reply with full conviction that there are none, even though they have never verified whether that is actually the case or not. The initial audience of the Quran (that is, those Arabs who were the first to hear the Quran being recited) tried to find discrepancies. The Quran itself encouraged this and understood it to be a natural and rational response to any new claim being made. Of course, after failing to find any discrepancies, they surrendered to the authority of the Quran. In contrast, one born into the faith assumes, or feels duty bound to assume, that there are no discrepancies within it because they have been taught from a young age that there cannot be any discrepancy in God's Book.

There is a big difference between these two approaches: The first is a genuine inquiry, and the other uncritical imitation. We have demonstrated the difference between them already. Recall we just discussed that if this message (of 'beating wives', 'taking slaves', and so on) came to you today in the twenty first century within the Western context, you would state: 'I cannot accept such commands. If you want me to accept them, then explain the rationale. If it makes sense to me (my reason), then I will accept it.' It is possible that you do not reject it outright at the onset, but you would certainly ask: 'I cannot accept it on the face of it, however if you give a reasonable explanation that appeals to me (my reason), I will accept it.'

Now can the Word of God be inconsistent with the human condition? The answer is obviously 'no'. Then how is it possible for His stipulations to lose their rational appeal? We know that these commandments of God were both rational and productive at the time of the revelation. However, the same commandments have lost their rational appeal in the contemporary era, for they no longer facilitate the growth of the individual and collectivity. Thus, it would seem the revelation and human condition are out of sync. How can this be possible when the Quran states, "So set your face to the religion as a *ḥanīf*, [that is, set it to] the nature (*fitra*) of Allah upon which He has moulded humankind; there is no substituting [completely] of Allah's creation..." (30:30)? Thus, Allah imbues this 'way' or 'nature' into existence, including humankind, that is, He fashions existence upon this 'nature'.

If the nature of existence is to fluctuate constantly, evolve, and liberate itself, then that means the human condition is also one of constant fluctuation, evolution, and liberation (or growth). It follows then that the 'forms' of societal regulations governing humans in the Quran are optimal only for the context of revelation and other similar contexts. In other words, the Quran provides 'forms' of the eternal truths (or 'essences') in and for its own context. This means the (apparent) literal meaning of verses prescribing societal regulations does not convey the regulations of God for contexts differing from the context of revelation; hence, the verses are to be read in their 'essential' capacity. If this is understood, then it will be clear that we are not moving away from the authority of the Word of God at all. We are merely saying that the said authority lies in the 'meaning' or 'spirit' of the Word principally, as opposed to the 'literal letter' of the Word.

The verse "This day, I have completed *your* religion (*dīn*) for *you…*" (5:3) makes perfect sense when read in the context in which it was revealed: It was revealed soon after the completion of the first hajj of the Muslims, which was also the first and last hajj of the blessed Prophet for he was soon to depart this world. In other words, this verse was revealed soon after the last devotional ceremony of the Muslims had been conveyed. Thus, the verse is merely stating: 'Islam is complete today in terms of its 'essence' (which is *islām* or 'surrendering to God') and its devotional regulations.' This 'completion' did not include the societal regulations of Islam for they were still being revealed after this point, instructing on new societal issues, so long as the Prophet was alive. In fact, 'completion' in the domain of societal regulations is impossible, for their formulation and reformulation is a continuous process that never ends so long as humankind exists in this cosmos.

We refer to an assertion held by Shia theologians generally to emphasise the unending nature of societal regulations: They argue that in theory the Prophet has the right to abrogate the regulations of the Quran and formulate new ones. They substantiate this by referencing the following verse: "And whatever the Messenger gives you, take it, and whatever he forbids, abstain from it." (59:7) Obviously, the abrogation in question is restricted to the domain of societal regulations, for no one is authorised to abrogate the worship of Allah and devotion to Him.

Both the body of societal regulations as a whole and its individual regulations can never be said to be 'completed' due to the ever-evolving nature of humankind and things. In fact, the societal regulations of the Quran can lose their efficacy to facilitate growth in individuals and collectivities belonging to contexts differing from the revelatory context. In such contexts, the literal appreciation of those verses of the Quran do not convey societal regulations; however, those verses do yield the 'essences' of the regulations whereby one can reformulate regulations safeguarding their 'essences'.

Perhaps the Mahdi will be charged with heresy because he will issue radically different societal regulations to those of seventh century Arabia we are accustomed to. Of course, his regulations will be the most humane and 'just', and yet he will be charged with changing the religion of his grandfather (as per the reports). Obviously, the Mahdi would never sanction anything that does not conform with the 'essence', which is *islām* or God-centricity, nor would he abolish devotional practices that engender a God-centric attitude and bestow the sense of Muslim identity to the Muslims. At most, he would modify the 'forms' of devotional practices as and when required (as his predecessors had done) to optimise their impact on the growth of individuals and collectivities, such as the 'form' of the fast. Thus, we are left with the societal regulations, and hence we can be certain that the Mahdi will change the societal regulations for which he will be charged with heresy. He will move away from the literal word of the Quran and fashion befitting 'forms' of the essences of those regulations. He will reinterpret the system of rights, the notion of punishment, and so on, if it has not already been done by the time of his arrival.

Another interpretation of the verse "This day, I have completed *your* religion (*dīn*) for *you*..." (5:3) is that it marks Imam Ali's appointment by the blessed Prophet at Ghadir Khumm as the authority (*mawlā*) after him. This makes sense too: Since flux is the nature of all things in existence, humankind will always face new challenges, and since new challenges can be existentially dangerous for a nascent community, it is only prudent that the most capable mind after the Prophet be made known to the people. In that way, the people and its leaders are aware that guidance to the best course of action is at hand should they want or require it.

To explain further: 'completion' can never signify the lock, stock, and barrel of societal regulations because any given society or collectivity can never stop changing, adding, and subtracting its regulations in accordance with the ever-evolving rational, moral, and spiritual needs of its members. Today we see people in the palms of our hands. Tomorrow we will be able to travel by thought. Everything has changed. We now have gender fluidity. Soon a man will be able to become a woman by the evening and revert back to being a man by the following day should he so choose. Things are changing very rapidly. Soon we will be traversing the galaxies. At that point, there will not be a Kaʿba to face, nor any sunrise or sunset. Which direction will we face to pray? What will the timings of prayers be? How will we perform hajj? Nothing will remain the same. These are all the bodily (outward) aspects of worship, and hence they can change as and when situations demand. Now how is one to reformulate that 'essence' for those of us who will be in space or on a different planet? No doubt, worship has an 'essence', but I repeat, how are we going to reformulate that 'essence'? It is for this reason that Ali ibn Abi Talib was appointed as the authority (*mawlā*). He was the best suited to refashion the 'essences' of regulations, and in so doing he would have left us with a body of Sharia reformulations. Successive Muslim scholars and jurists would have studied his reformulations and benefited immensely: they would have realised that the interpretation of the Quran must be as fluid as the evolving human being, and they would have been able to extract the methods and principles for refashioning regulations.

Therefore, Imam Ali's appointment was to ensure that the spiritual and moral essences of the Quran and the Prophet's teachings were safeguarded within the nascent Muslim community, as opposed to their forms. Hence, his appointment went beyond political remit – it was to uphold the essences of the Quranic and Prophetic teachings.

I will gesture at one of the tools in the method of deriving the 'essence' of regulations. I term it 'hypothetical Islam'. Imagine a future world in which we are able to teleport ourselves from London to Sydney in the blinking of an eye. What would that mean for 'shortening prayers' and 'breaking the fast'? Hypothetical thought experiments assist us in understanding and extrapolating the real values within regulations. Imagine if the severed hand of a thief can be regrown immediately by advanced cloning technology. In this case, what purpose does the severing of the hand serve? Here, we begin to understand that the cutting of hands was not done for its own sake; rather, it served a purpose which was to curtail corruption and protect society. If hands can be regrown in a matter of hours, then these purposes (of curtailing corruption and protecting society) will not be achieved by merely cutting the hands of thieves. Thus, we understand that 'cutting hands' is one of many possible 'forms' that can be envisaged for protecting society from thieves. Hence, this regulation of the Quran is not eternal, immutable, or universal in its literal capacity.

Today, antagonists accuse Muslims and the blessed Prophet of condoning and practicing paedophilia because of our insistence on the 'completeness' of Islam as a legal regulative system. Historically, we can be fairly certain that the age of Lady Ayesha was not less than 18 years. However, it is undeniable that Arabs, like Indians, ancients Greeks, and pre-modern Europeans, had a culture of marrying young girls, but it did not constitute 'paedophilia' by seventh century Arabian standards, or even by pre-modern standards generally, for such a notion did not exist until recently: The moral sophistication of the human community in this regard has only just begun to flower; perhaps its onset can be said to be the signing of the universal declaration of human rights in December 1948 by forty-eight countries. In any case, the notion of the innocence of children and their rights is a very recent development in the timeline of the history of human beings.

Think about this: If I were to say, 'This child killed that man with a gun. Therefore, this child has committed murder', I would be told that for any 'killing' to classify as 'murder', the killer must know and be aware of what he is doing during the act; in other words, murder is 'the wilful, or premeditated, killing of one human by another'. Accordingly, an undiscerning child can never qualify as a 'murderer' because it does not understand what it means to take a life unjustly. Thus, a child's act of killing someone does not qualify as 'murder' because the adjectives 'wilful' and 'premeditated' can never be ascribed to the act.

Technically, paedophilia is a medical diagnosis given to an adult or older adolescent who experiences a primary or exclusive sexual attraction to prepubescent children, that is, children aged 13 or under. In pre-modern societies, which includes European societies, pubescent girls and boys were considered to be of marriageable age, that is, they could be married as soon as they could conceive. Typically, girls were able to start conceiving between the ages of 9 and 13 years in those days. Strictly speaking, this does not qualify as 'paedophilia' in the technical medical sense, but it does qualify as 'paedophilia' as understood by people at large. The common usage of 'paedophilia' today refers to an adult's sexual attraction towards pre-pubescent and pubescent girls and boys, and post-pubescent teenagers. Hence sexual relations between an adult and a teenager are morally bad and illegal today. There is no doubt that this norm is consistent with the evolution and growth of societies today. However, in pre-modern societies, the marriage of an adult to either a pubescent or a post-pubescent teenager was not deemed to be morally bad or a moral vice; on the contrary, to marry a girl as soon as she was able to conceive was considered a moral act, for it allowed her to fulfil one of her God given functions. Therefore, such marriages in pre-modern societies cannot be classified as 'paedophilia' in both the technical and popular senses.

The way to reply to antagonists who say that Islam ordained slavery is to ask whether it was frowned upon in the societal milieu and context of seventh century Arabia specifically and the pre-modern world generally to the same degree as it is today? If the answer is 'yes' (that is, it was frowned upon in those times to the same degree as it is today), then we can point the finger of blame at the Quran and assert that it was ordaining something inconsistent with the 'human nobility' and dignity of the time. However, if the answer is 'no' because pre-modern societies were not as morally sophisticated as societies today, then it is conceivable for a pre-modern society to be as moral as it could be and yet permit slavery despite it being frowned upon by many of its leaders. The Quran cannot be blamed for anything that is considered indecent and inconsistent with human rights and human dignity by today's standards. There is no doubt that slavery is wrong by today's standards, and yet it was tolerated in that context due to the limitations of that context, and hence it was acknowledged as a societal phenomenon and a feature of that society.

It was considered normal and 'just' a hundred years ago for women to not be given the right to vote. Today, countries that do not allow women to vote are regarded as 'backward'. Things have changed over the last hundred years; there has been moral growth and sophistication. Ten years ago, women were paid less than men for doing the same job, and it was deemed to be perfectly fine and 'just'. Today, the inequality of pay based on gender is viewed as an injustice in the West: Why should women be paid less than men? Ten years ago, it was not considered as unjust; however, it is unjust ten years on. Now this does not mean that people in the West were bad, barbaric, unsophisticated, and immoral ten years ago. The need for change is simply the effect of a continually changing context and the constant evolution of 'human nobility'.

Today, it is fine to have servants. In a hundred years from now, the notion of 'humans serving humans' or 'humans having human servants' will be abhorred in the same way we abhor slavery today. Existence is constantly fluctuating, resulting in moral growth and sophistication; hence, these debates will never stop. What is important is that there be an equilibrium between morality and the limitations of the context whereby things make sense in their own context. Thus, the rule is: If something makes sense in its own context, then it is perfectly fine. Does it still make sense in this context? No. Then that particular regulation or norm has now passed its 'optimal efficacy' date and needs to be renewed.

The Quran was well ahead of its time. Its injunctions propelled the community forward in a progressive direction. It declared that women had the same spiritual status as men at a time when the prevalent belief throughout the world was that women were deficient as humans in comparison to men. The Quran gave them rights of ownership, inheritance, and divorce. The Quran also tried to make the institution of slavery and the treatment of slaves as humane as possible. It respected their freedom of choice and declared them as having the same spiritual status as free men. In fact, it was understood by everyone who heard the Quran that it was possible for God to be closer to a slave than to his/her master. Hence, the Quran effectively deconstructed the master/slave dichotomy for it rendered the differences between slaves and their masters as arbitrary and unreal. In view of this and the norms instituted to govern the master/slave relationship, it is clear that the Quran intended to initiate the process of the liberation of slaves. The Quran also gave orphans their rights and institutionalised a welfare system to look after the poor and vulnerable. Similarly, it delineated the rights of parents, children, neighbours, and wayfarers to name but a few. It is a great tragedy that we Muslims are stuck in seventh century Arabia as a result of having ascribed 'finality' to the societal regulations of the Quran, instead of furthering the emancipatory trajectory initiated by it.Religion appeals to one and all when it is in sync with the human condition and intuition. Religious teachings ought to liberate us and bring us to the fullness of our existence. Religion ought to give us a sense of purpose, fulfilment and belonging, and a beautiful spiritual orientation. At a practical level, religion must be very productive and not unjust. We are attracted to religions when they convey such values in their teachings. Do Christianity, Judaism, Hinduism, and Islam, have that appeal at present? We find that the aspect of spiritual orientation towards God in all these religions attracts us; however, their societal regulations do not cater for the needs and demands of a progressive and pluralistic human community, and hence they do not appeal to us at all in that regard.

As stated previously, the instructive 'forms' of the Sharia are of two types: devotional and societal. Inaccurate 'forms' of devotional regulations do not do significant harm to the individual and collectivity in general, hence their inaccuracy is not serious. However, the case is not the same for inaccurate 'forms' of societal regulations, for they push people away from religion altogether. The detestability we feel regarding such 'forms' stems either from the fact that they are based on the ideology of the *exclusivity* of the Truth and salvation (which is effectively the belief in the superiority of the members of one religion or sect over all others), or from the fact that they are based on the rights given to different categories of people in seventh century Muslim Medina. The universalisation and application of the rights, regulations, and norms of seventh century Muslim Medina to today's context without any modification, results in unequal rights being afforded to different categories of people. Such rights are deemed to be unequal based on today's evolved standard of morality, and hence they are unacceptable to most people. People perceive the Sharia as privileging the Muslim male above all other categories of people for no reason other than the fact that he is 'Muslim' and 'male'. Consequently, they consider many of the societal norms and regulations of the Sharia as being self-evidently and inherently unequal; hence, they perceive the religion as regressive and its community of followers as being closed-minded, irrational, and immoral.

The Quran provides fundamental principles that were meant to be applied in every era to determine a befitting system of societal regulations for humankind as *humankind*; in other words, the Quran mentions certain principles that are to be the basis of all legal systems irrespective of the faith of people. They are 'human nobility', 'the principle of justice' (the appreciation of which in any given time and place depends on the degree of growth of 'human nobility' of the collectivity in that time and place), and the principles of non-coercion and the sacredness of human life. The problem is that we have attached the label of 'sacred' to the totality of societal regulations in the Sharia without distinguishing the 'sacred' element within them. Instead of realising that it is 'the principle of justice', 'human nobility' and the principles of non-coercion and the sacredness of human life that are 'sacred', we have sacralised their 'forms' which were revealed over fourteen hundred years ago to the Muslims of Medina.

The following verse of the Quran serves as a textual evidence for the mutability of Sharia formulations:

> *Whatever verse We abrogate or cause to be forgotten, We bring one better than it or the like of it; do you not know that Allah is Powerful over everything? (2:106)*

This verse refers to the occurrence of the phenomenon of abrogation within God's Own communication, the Quran. The question is: How can any part in the eternal Word of God be abrogated? Surely it must be true and relevant until the Day of Judgement? Surprisingly, that's not how God sees it; He understands and respects that His creation is in flux resulting in contextual changes and different rational, moral, and spiritual needs of people at different times and places; hence, He issues different formulations to ensure the optimal growth of the individual and collectivity. Is it not significant that the Quran not only mentions the occurrence of this phenomenon but also leaves examples of abrogated verses inside it?

The phenomenon of the abrogation of parts of the previous *sharias* by subsequent ones is another support for the mutability of Sharia formulations. Why did Prophet Musa make additions to Prophet Ibrahim's *sharia*? Prophet Ibrahim's *sharia* was minimalistic and inadequate in catering for the needs of Prophet Musa's community. Why did Prophet Isa say to the Israelites: 'I have come to make some things lawful that were forbidden to you?' (3:50) Why did Prophet Muhammad abrogate many regulations and practices in the *sharia* of Prophet Musa and add other new ones? Why did the Quran exclude the practice of stoning to death as a punishment?

Did any of these blessed prophets abrogate the 'essences' of the regulations? Did they instruct their respective audiences to not be "godlike" and "God-centred", or to be indecent and immoral? Did they instruct their respective communities to behave contrary to their sense of human values? Obviously, the blessed prophets could never abrogate these 'essential' aspects of religion. They only abrogated the regulations of previous *sharias* that had become outdated and hence were no longer fulfilling their 'essences': such regulations were either not facilitating the rational, moral, and spiritual growth of the individual and collectivity, or they were less than optimal in facilitating their growth. Consequently, the blessed prophets refashioned such regulations in accordance with their own respective contexts ensuring that the 'essences' were being fulfilled and thereby safeguarding them.

The Quran says:

> *Indeed, We have ennobled the Children of Adam, and We carry them in land and sea, and We have provided them with good sustenance, and We have favoured them above many of those We have created with a marked favour. (17:70)*

"We have ennobled the Children of Adam." Our collective 'nobility' (which is the innate sense of compassion, decency, and godliness within humankind) is being refined continually in a similar way to how a growing human being becomes nobler with age and experience. When people ask me, 'Why are you against abortion?', my response is that despite conceding philosophically to the possibility that the foetus might not have a right to live in itself because it cannot claim that right, our *nobility* will give it that right, nonetheless. Similarly, a goat does not have the right to live when I choose to eat it, however when humankind ripens and becomes sophisticated, our *nobility* will not allow us to slaughter and eat that being. This is who we are, and this is the way we are. You cannot take a person and start flogging them in public. Human dignity does not allow for that anymore. We do not cut people's hands off anymore. Our 'human nobility' and dignity do not allow us to humiliate anybody like that. The blessed Prophet formulated regulations with the lowest common denominator in mind. You do not have to tell a noble person not to steal; their nobility does not allow them to do so. Similarly, you do not have to tell a noble soul to speak the truth; again, their nobility does not allow them to do otherwise.

Therefore, the verse "This day, I have completed your religion (*dīn*) for you…" (5:3) signifies the 'completion' of the conveyance of the devotional regulations of Islam and hence the Muslim religious identity. It also happened to mark the occasion of the announcement of Imam Ali as the most qualified to lead the community after the blessed Prophet in terms of both spiritual and worldly aspects of Islam.

Now let us consider the following verse: "And whoever desires a religion (*dīn*) other than *islām*, it will never be accepted from him; and in the Hereafter he will be one of the losers." (3:85) What is the meaning of 'acceptance'? Think about this carefully. The following example will clarify one of its meanings. Imagine that a teacher says to the student: 'If you do the homework on anything other than an A4 sheet of paper, I will not accept it.' The student is the 'Einstein' of his time, and he writes the homework on a scrap piece of paper and submits it to the teacher, and of course it includes his ground-breaking formulas and theories. Now will the teacher say, 'Cast it into the fire for he has not written it on an A4 sheet of paper, and so I will not accept it from him!'? Obviously not, for what he has written on the tiny sheet of paper is the greatest breakthrough humankind has ever achieved even though the cosmetic part of the requirement of the homework was not right. Thus, the teacher will not cast it into the fire.

So now we can understand what is meant by 'non-acceptance'? It means that an action will not bear any fruits. What does Allah want from all these practices? He wants us to grow inwardly and become godly creatures. Thus, when Allah states that He will not accept the choice of a person who chooses a *dīn* other than *islām*, He means that any other *dīn* will not bear any fruit. The 'fruit' in question is proximity to God and godly self-realisation. Thus, a *dīn* other than *islām* will not result in proximity to God. It is only the *dīn* of *islām* (which as we know is to surrender one's ego to the Source of all beauty, the Point of utmost glory, and the Peak of human aspiration) that will bear the fruits of proximity to God and godly self-realisation and hence be accepted.

Somebody asked Imam Ali: 'How do I know if my prayers have been accepted?' The Imam responded with a narration from the blessed Prophet: 'If you find that you have become more refined in your spirituality and morality upon completing your prayers (that is, if you see that you are a better person), then that prayer has been accepted. If you do not find that goodness in your soul, then that particular prayer has gone to waste.' In other words, if the prayer bears fruits in one's character, then one should know that it has been accepted. Note how the criterion he gave for the acceptance of prayers did not include the correctness of the 'form' or method. He did not say: 'Your prayers are accepted if and only if you do *takbir* in this way and not that way, or if you fold your arms like this and not like that, or if you leave your arms open in this manner and not that, or if you recite in proper Arabic with *makhraj* (correct pronunciation)'.

The word *dīn* in the above verse and other verses (such as "Indeed, the *dīn* with Allah is islām" – 3:19) does not refer to the Sharia or regulative system that is set in stone; rather, it denotes a way of life that firstly is orientated towards Allah exclusively and secondly understands God's Will to be His desire for humankind to perform the best possible course of action in any given situation. In other words, the way of life that is lived for God and His proximity (*dīn*) requires us to choose the most ethical course of action in all societal interactions. For instance, 'the *dīn* of Allah' demands that today's trade and commerce be ethical. Now to ensure the most ethical course of action is taken with respect to trading, we will not look at what the regulations on buying and selling were in seventh century Muslim Arabia only; rather, we will also analyse the phenomenon of trading as it is today in the twenty-first century from as many perspectives as possible in light of ethical principles, all the while calculating hypothetical moral implications. For instance, we will ask the following questions during our analysis of our businesses: 'Is any degree of slave labour involved in the production of materials used by the business?', 'Is the production of goods injurious to the environment?', and 'Is there any injustice being done to anyone in this trade or business?' If the answers to such questions are in the affirmative, then the business is immoral and hence prohibited irrespective of how lucrative it is and how beneficial it may be to the national interest. If it takes away the rights of poor people, ruins the environment, or has detrimental impact on the mineral, plant, and animal kingdoms, it is not ethical. Such considerations are pertinent to our context today, hence the new regulations of Islam must address them and provide guidelines based on ethical principles so that businesses, communities, societies, and nation states can discern what is permitted and what is not.

Lecture Six

The *Milla* of Ibrahim, and *Dīn*

In the past few lectures, we have been analysing the usage of the words *dīn* and 'islām' in the Quran. The word 'islām' has been used in two ways: the first refers to the *perennial* and fluid 'religion (*dīn*) of God' or *islām*, and the second to the organised 'formal' religion, that is, Islam. We referred to verses of the Quran demonstrating that *dīn* is a singular reality and truth which has been revealed time and again in different 'forms' according to the rational, moral, and spiritual demands of its audience and context. We also discussed verses equating 'the *dīn* of Allah' with *islām* essentially, which is the wholesome surrender to God and His communication. We concluded that 'the *dīn* of Allah' consists of an 'essence' and a 'form': the 'essence' is God-centricity, and the 'form' is a particular religion's devotional regulations (which bestow an attitude of God-centricity and the sense of religious identity to those who perform them), and its societal regulations (which are in a state of flux and hence in need of constant monitoring and potential revision to ensure they remain optimal in assisting the growth of the individual and collectivity).

Towards the end of the last lecture, we were analysing the following verse: "And whoever desires a religion (*dīn*) other than *islām*, it will never be accepted from him; and in the Hereafter he will be one of the losers." (3:85) We discussed that 'non-acceptance' means 'not bearing fruits'; in other words, 'non-acceptance' means 'not attaining salvation', and so the meaning of the verse is: surrendering to other than God does not assist in the culmination of godliness and the attainment of salvation.

The Quran states that previous prophets and their respective communities performed prayers (*ṣalāt*), paid the poor-rate (*zakāt*) and kept fasts (*ṣawm*). For instance, Prophet Ismail "… commanded his family to perform *ṣalāt* and pay *zakāt*…" (19:55), Prophet Isa said, "… and He (God) has enjoined on me *ṣalāt* and *zakāt* so long as I live." (19:31), and the past prophets generally "… upheld *ṣalāt* and paid *zakāt*." (21:73) Regarding fasting, it states, "O you who believe, fasting is prescribed for you, as it was prescribed for those before you …." (2:183), concerning the direction of prayers, it says, "And for every [group], there is a direction to which they face…" (2:148), and regarding the pilgrimage of every religion and its rituals, "To every [religious] community, We have given a sacred ritual which they are to perform …" (22:67) Thus, we discern that the religions (*adyān*) of all the prophets were the same inasmuch as the spiritual component or 'essence' of each was God-centricity, and yet they differed from each other insofar as the 'forms' of the regulations of each differed from the others. The Quran states the truth and reality of this explicitly: "We have assigned a law and a path (*minhāj*) to each [group of people]…". (5:48)

The Quran contrasts 'the *dīn* of Allah' with the '*dīn*' of the *kuffār* of Mecca: "[Say O Muhammad,] for you is your *dīn*, and for me is my *dīn*." (109:6) We understand from this that '*dīn*' consists of a set of beliefs and practices (corresponding to and based on those beliefs). Obviously, 'the *dīn* of Allah' or *islām* is based on 'surrender to Allah', whereas those *adyān* (religions or ways of life) that are contrary to 'the *dīn* of Allah' are based on 'surrender to *other* than God'. The effect of this 'essential' difference is the adherence to godly and ungodly practices respectively. This distinction is made apparent by verses referencing 'the *milla* of

Ibrahim' or 'the creed of Ibrahim'. According to lexicologists, the word *milla* signifies 'a way of belief and practice in respect of religion (*dīn*)'.

Consider the following verses: "And strive hard in [the way of] Allah, [such] a striving as is due to Him; He has chosen you and has not laid upon you a hardship in *dīn*; the *milla* of your father Ibrahim; He named you *muslims* before and in this [revelation]…" (22:78) This verse states that the *dīn* of Muhammad is 'the *milla* of Ibrahim', that is, 'the creed or set of beliefs and practices of Ibrahim'. As we will see, 'the *milla* of Ibrahim' is the archetype of all monotheistic religions.

The following verse, "… rather [ours is] the creed (*milla*) of Ibrahim, a *ḥanīf*; he was not of the polytheists" (2:135), conveys the central belief of 'the *milla* of Ibrahim', which is *tawḥid*, and differentiates it from other creeds (*millal*) explicitly and their 'formal' devotional practices and societal systems by implication.

The Quran makes reference to an ungodly *milla* in the verse pertaining to the Youths of the Cave who were conversing after they had awoken: "If they [the people outside of the cave] should get knowledge of you, they will stone you or they will turn you back to their *milla*." (18:20) Here, "their *milla*" signifies their belief in deities other than Allah and their practices of worshiping idols and adopting lifestyles other than those of 'the *milla* of Ibrahim' (or the archetypical religion of Ibrahim).

The following verse uses the word *dīn* to signify another meaning: "… He [Yusuf] could not have taken his brother in accordance with 'the *dīn* of the king' except that Allah willed…" (12:76) Here, 'the *dīn* of the king' signifies the 'formal' socio-political-economic system of Egypt that was based on their religious assumptions and fundamental beliefs. Obviously, Prophet Yusuf did not worship idols, and yet he abided by the norms and regulations of 'the *dīn* of the king of Egypt', that is, the socio-political-economic system which was under the authority of the king of Egypt.

Thus, every *dīn* (religion or way of life) is based on certain fundamental beliefs. According to the Quran, religions or 'ways of life' have either been God-centric and monotheistic, that is, they have been based on 'the archetypical religion (*milla*) of Ibrahim', resulting in virtuous God-centred devotional practices and just social orders, or they have been polytheistic in nature resulting in idol-centred rituals and unjust societal setups. The Quran substantiates this in the following verses: "And when they commit an indecent act, they say, 'we found our fathers doing it and Allah enjoined it upon us.' Say, 'Allah does not ordain indecency....'" (7:28) and "Indeed, Allah commands justice and generosity, and giving to kinsfolk; and He forbids indecency and the reprehensible and oppression...". (16:90)

In conclusion, the verse "For you is your *dīn*, and for me is my *dīn*." (109:6) refers to two distinct and diametrically opposed *form*-based outlooks and their practices. The opposition between them is due to the foundational beliefs and assumptions held by each. The Abrahamic faiths are the same 'in essence' because they are merely diverse 'forms' of the *perennial* and 'archetypical religion (*milla*) of Ibrahim'. The Quran confirms this understanding constantly. Consider the following verses which address those followers of all three Abrahamic faiths who were claiming superiority over members of other faiths and religions:

> *It [the admittance to Paradise] is not [in accordance with] your wishful thinking [O believers] nor the thinking of the People of the Book. Whoever does evil, he will be recompensed with it ... And whoever performs righteous deeds, male or female, and are faithful, these shall enter Paradise... Who is better in dīn than one who surrenders his whole self to Allah and is doer of good (muḥsin) and follows the milla of Ibrahim, a ḥanīf... (4:123-5)*

Notice how the verse refers to "whoever", among the People of the Book and the followers of the Prophet, "performs righteous deeds... and are faithful", without specifying any particular religion, sect, or faith, "shall enter Paradise". Then it states that the best *dīn* (religion or way of life) is 'surrendering the whole of one's self to God' (that is, *islām*), which is the product of following 'the archetypical religion (*milla*) of Ibrahim'.

> *"And who would turn away from the milla of Ibrahim except one who has fooled himself... When his (Ibrahim's) Lord said to him, 'Surrender.' He replied, 'I surrender [myself] to the Lord of the Universe.' And Ibrahim enjoined his sons with this, and [so did] Yaqub: 'My sons, indeed Allah has chosen for you the [true] religion (dīn); therefore, do not die save as muslimūn (those surrendered to Him or in the state of islām)." (2:130-2)*

Therefore, the connection between 'the *milla* of Ibrahim' and the various 'forms' of 'the *dīn* of Allah' is that any given 'form', which is an expression of *islām* in and for a particular context, has the fundamental beliefs of 'the *milla* of Ibrahim' at its core. Similarly, the various 'forms' of 'the *dīn* of polytheism' are expressions of 'the *dīn* of polytheism' in and for a particular context and have at their core the fundamental beliefs of 'the *milla* of polytheism'. To reiterate, *dīn* (religion or way of life) is the 'formulation' of theological doctrine, and devotional and societal regulations in and for a particular context, and it has the fundamental beliefs of 'the archetypical religion of Ibrahim' at its base.

It should be noted that all the discussions in the Quran are based on, or centre around, one fundamental distinction: 'the friend of God' and 'the enemy of God'. Accordingly, *dīn* is either 'the *dīn* of God', or it is 'the *dīn* of other than God'. 'The *dīn* of God' leads to godliness and salvation, and 'the *dīn* of other than God' leads to alienation from God and damnation. This is because the *dīn* we choose causes us to evolve and actualise our human potential in accordance with its core beliefs and worldview.

The other meaning of the word *dīn* in the Quran is 'recompense' as in the verse: "the Owner of the Day of Reckoning (*māliki yawmi al-dīn*)." (1:4) The recompense being referred to here will be given to humans in accordance with the deeds they performed in their worldly lives. The Quran often expresses that the people of Paradise will 'receive reward for what they have earned' (see for instance 45:14) and the people of Hell will 'taste what they have earned' (see for instance 39:24). The Quran employs the terms of *fawz* (success) and *khusr* (failure or loss) in relation to those who attain salvation and taste damnation respectively: "… And whoever is removed away from the Fire and admitted to Paradise, he indeed is *successful*…" (3:185) and "… Say, 'Indeed, the *losers* are those who shall have *lost* themselves and their families on the Day of Resurrection…" (39:15) Upon reading the verses of the Quran narrating the nature of the Day of Judgement, including the fact that the polytheists will be asked to call upon those they used to associate with God, it is clear that the Day of Judgement (*yawm al-dīn*) is a period of reckoning wherein every soul will see the impact of the *dīn* they chose to follow upon this earth in their very selves; in other words, each soul will see what they have become as a result of their choice of *dīn*.

The root letters of the word *dīn*, which are *da-ya-na*, can also be read as *dayn* meaning 'a debt' from which the word *dīn* in the sense of 'judgement' is derived. Hence, the Quran's choice of employing the word *dīn* repeatedly to refer to the Final Day is to signify that the Reckoning is the consequence of a covenant we made with God in the life prior to this one in which we committed ourselves to follow 'His *dīn*' (religion or way of life) during our lives on this earth; in other words, humankind has taken a responsibility upon itself to fulfil a task upon this earth, and hence this worldly life of ours is a debt.

The Prophet of Allah would stand long hours at night worshipping Allah, lamenting, and weeping before Him. His feet would swell. Lady Ayesha would say to him, 'Ya Rasul Allah', and then recite the verse, "that Allah may forgive you of what preceded of your sins and what are to follow…" (48:2) The blessed Prophet would respond: 'O Ayesha, should I not be a thankful servant of Allah?' What did he mean by saying this? Incidentally, the verse states that Allah has forgiven all his sins, ¬both past and future. Today's Muslims would find it very odd that a verse of the Quran states that the blessed Prophet had past sins and will have future sins, but that is another discussion. In any case, the Prophet answers Lady Ayesha: 'Should I not be a thankful servant of Allah? This opportunity of life is a favour of Allah upon me. How can I ever pay it back?' What a phenomenal understanding the Prophet is presenting here: Every moment of this life is a debt to Allah! It is generally believed that Allah created us on this earth for the first time, and that we had no individual existence in other realms prior to this worldly life. In other words, He has created us in this world, made us act out our lives, and after that He will judge us. How can such a theology make sense to anyone?

Think about this carefully: Allah instructs, "Be grateful to Me and to your parents." (31:14) I ask: 'Why O Lord?' Allah answers: 'I have made this beautiful earth for you with its gravity, air, and water. I have made the sun to give you warmth. I have grown plants as sustenance for you and your animals. I have made arks for you to sail upon.' We may reply: 'O Allah, had You not created me in the first place, would You have needed to make all these things for me? O Lord, had You not made me with lungs, You would not have needed to make air for me. Had You not made my life contingent to the sun, would You have had to create the sun for me? O Lord, if You have made me with a stomach that gets hungry, then of course I will need to eat and drink. How then is it a favour upon me, O Lord?'

Then we may continue, 'O Allah, with all due respect, who asked You to create me in the first place? It is You Who has created me in a state of dire need, and then You Yourself fulfil that need. How is that a favour upon me, O Lord?' To further emphasise the problem, let us look at how God's command of being grateful to parents is illogical based on our current theological assumptions. One can say to their parents: 'Why should I thank you, O parents? You need not have brought me into this world. Now that you have brought me into this world, I am in need of sustenance, and so you sustain me from your bosom. I am in need of clothing, and so you clothe me. I am in need of food, and so you feed me. I am an infant and cannot do anything, and so you have to cater for my needs. You have brought me into this world, and so the onus is on you to nurture me. In all of this, where is the bestowal and favour? Why should I thank you? In fact, you should be thankful that I do not take you to court and sue you for bringing me into this hellish world. Who asked you to bring me into this world?' Think about this carefully.

Can our current theological understanding – that 'I was nothing, and then one day God decided to create me!' – be correct if its implication is what we have just been through, namely that life is not actually a favour, and as such 'thanking God' is not warranted? Does this not indicate that our belief is a naïve assumption? Surely, we are entitled to ask God: 'I was nothing, and then one day you decided to create me. After that, You gave me all these things to fulfil my needs. Everybody says this is a favour, but I ask You, O Lord, how is this a favour? In fact, due to their transgressive nature, humans have made this world a hellish place to live prior to my birth, and yet despite knowing the hellish state of this world, You created me to reside in it anyway. O Lord, how is this a favour?'

Allah says in the Quran:

> *Say, 'He has power to send punishment upon you from above or from beneath your feet, or to confuse you [and divide you] into discordant factions and make you taste the violence of one another.' See how We explain Our communications [in various ways], so that they may understand. (6:65)*

How many people have died because of natural disasters like the Tsunami, floods, and earthquakes? How many have they destroyed? A hundred thousand? How many people have we destroyed in the name of our sects? Syria has been raised to the ground. How barbaric are we? The greatest form of punishment upon humankind has been the disputes we have amongst ourselves. Look at the way we have killed each other. In light of this, we ask: 'O God, You brought me into this hellish world with a defective nature. I suffer in it, and when I do rejoice, it is at the expense of other peoples' suffering. How can You expect me to thank You for bringing me into this sort of world? Furthermore, according to the religious teachings, I have no hope beyond this world, because after we die, most of us are going to Hell directly. In fact, prior to Hell, I must endure the ordeal of the grave and the pain and torment of the intermediate realms (*al-barāzikh*), at the end of which is the Day of Judgement (*yawm al-qiyāma*). O Lord, why should I thank You for any of this?'

Now all of this (that is, this current life, the post-mortmic life, and the eschatological truths mentioned in the Quran) only make sense when we realise that we are in a state of *debt* to Allah. A debt exists only after we have asked for something and a contract or a deal has been made. Therefore, Allah has not *sent* us to this world in the simplistic way we have assumed. According to the Quran, we have *asked* for this life and made a deal:

> *Indeed, We offered the Trust to the heavens, the earth, and the mountains, yet they refused to undertake it and were afraid of it; and humankind undertook it. Surely, he is unjust and ignorant.* (33:72)

When the verse states that "Indeed, We offered the Trust to the heavens, the earth, and the mountains", it assumes we know it means that the Trust was offered to the 'inhabitants' of the heavens, earth, and mountains. However, their respective inhabitants are not humans like us. This means God has created all of this for us because we asked for it. We asked for an opportunity to worship Him and be like Him. Therefore, this world and every breath is a debt to Allah, for Allah did not have to create any of this. We desired this opportunity of life to gain a grand status. Accordingly, Allah says of the human: "…he may be grateful or ungrateful." (76:3)

In view of this, our parents are mere passages for us to come into this world; moreover, it seems we have chosen them as the means of arriving into this world. Our mothers destroyed their health because we wanted to come here, and both parents sacrificed their lives to raise us into adults. Hence, Allah honours parents by placing the instruction to be kind towards them immediately after commanding His Own worship:

Your Lord has decreed that you should worship none but Him, and [that you show] kindness to your parents. If either or both of them reach old age with you, say no word that shows impatience with them, and do not be harsh with them, but speak to them respectfully (17:23)

The following verse of the Quran also refers to the fact that we made a deal in asking for this life, and hence we are in 'debt':

And [remember] when your Lord brought forth from the Children of Adam, from their loins, their descendants and made them testify of themselves, [saying], "Am I not your Lord?" They said, "Yes, we testify!" – lest you should say on the Day of Resurrection, "Verily, we were unaware of this." (7:172)

Therefore, we are indebted to God for our lives in this world.

Read the following verse of the Quran: "Did I not make a covenant with you, O Children of Adam, that you should not serve Satan? Indeed, he is your open enemy." (36:60) When did we make this pact? Since this event is part of our history, it is a part of our existential condition, as explained in last year's lecture series. There are numerous verses in the Quran alluding to oaths we have taken and pacts we have made. Despite having forgotten them, the Quran reminds us of them because we will remember them all on the Last Day. These oaths and pacts we have undertaken and made in our past are the reason for our being held to account on the Day of Judgement, during which testimonies and Scribes will be presented detailing whether we were successful in executing them or not. In other words, the reason for recompensating our deeds and actions in the Hereafter is because of pacts we made in a pre-worldly state or life. The Quran mentions the response of the inhabitants of Hell when they are asked why they were driven to Hell: "They shall say: We were not of those who prayed; nor did we feed the poor... and we used to deny the Day of Judgment." (74:43-46) Again, the Quran states that "... On that Day, man shall remember, but what of his recollection? He will say: 'Ah, would that I had sent [some provision] for [this] my life!'" (89:23-24)

Coming back to the notion of *dīn* in the sense of 'religion' or 'way of life', we understand in light of the preceding discussions that the phrase 'the *dīn* of Allah' refers to the way of life resulting in the fullness of our existence and its completion, and that pledging to follow this '*dīn* of Allah' seems to be the only pact we have made.

We need to ask ourselves the following question: What do we take from this world of ours? When you are lowered into your grave, your body will wither into the dust from whence it was formed. Nothing shall remain of the palaces, prestige, wealth, and knowledge you accrued. When you go back to God, the only thing you will take is yourself. What will be the state of yourself when this happens? Will you be a fully actualised soul?

Therefore, you are in a constant state of debt, and you yourself are the recompense. Your soul is either successful in itself or it is a failure. Our own selves are the punishment. Allah says that the punishment of Hell is what you have earned for yourselves. (10:52) Similarly, those who enter Paradise receive what is appropriate for what they had earned. (52:21) When we return to Allah, all we take is what we have become. Thereafter, Allah will pass the Decisive Judgment on the Day of Qiyāma. So *dīn* means the way in which we go about actualising ourselves and paying back the debt to Allah. Our souls have the potential in this bodily life to be actualised in either a godly or an ungodly manner, and consequently that actualised state is reflected as salvation or damnation respectively.

Consider the following verse once again: "He it is Who sent His Messenger with guidance and 'the religion of the Truth', that He might cause it to prevail over all religions, though the polytheists may be averse." (9:33) The previous verse ends with the phrase, "though the *unbelievers* are averse". ("They desire to put out the light of Allah with their mouths, and Allah refuses [for that to happen] but rather [He wills] that He completes His light, though the unbelievers are averse." 9:32) To make sense of the meaning of this verse (9:33), we need to understand the context at the time of its revelation. The Quran uses the words *kuffār* (sing. *kāfir*) and *mushrik* to refer to the Meccans who opposed the blessed Prophet. The former did not mean 'those who rejected the belief in God', rather it denoted 'one wilfully opposed to God'. Thus, those the Quran termed as '*kāfirūn*' or '*kuffār*' were not people who disbelieved in God, rather they assented to the existence of God and then deliberately sought to oppose Him.

Similarly, those the Quran termed as *mushrikūn* were not people who naïvely associated others with God, rather they were people advocating obedience to other gods as a means of opposing Allah's commandments (see Sūra al-Anʿām and other places). They were able to institute every 'form' of immorality by referencing their gods; they would say, "... Allah enjoined it upon us...", and Allah responds, "... Indeed, Allah does not ordain indecency; do you say about Allah what you do not know?'" (7:28). Thus, the terms *mushrik* and *kuffār* referred to people who defied God in the name of the divine or the unseen itself. By doing this, they were effectively saying that either the God of Muhammad, Musa, and Isa is a false God, or that their gods have given them supremacy over others and license to commit all manners of injustices and exploitations as and when they want. Hence, Allah asks them: "Do you say about Allah what you do not know?'" (7:28), or in other words, 'How can God ordain indecency' and 'How can God ordain injustice?' Here, God is addressing the faculty of intuition within their souls directly: 'Look deep within yourselves, for then you will know that God can never ordain such things'.

Therefore, the verse "He it is Who sent His Messenger with guidance and 'the religion of the Truth', that He might cause it to prevail over all religions, though the polytheists may be averse." (9:33) means that the Prophet would inaugurate 'the *dīn* of the Truth', which is 'Islam' or his 'form' of *islām*, and that it ('the *dīn* of the Truth') would be an overarching system subsuming all 'forms' of the good life within it. It ('the *dīn* of the Truth') would be a very broad and dynamic system including and celebrating the diversity and plurality of all 'forms' provided they are God-centric. Hence, the Quran always emphasises, "… Say, 'We believe in what was revealed to us and in what was revealed to you; our God and your God are one [and the same]…" (29:46) and

> *Say [O Muhammad], 'O People of the Book, you are upon nothing until you establish the Torah and Gospel, and that which has been sent down to you from your Lord.' And what has been revealed to you from your Lord [O Muhammad] is sure to increase many of them in their insolence and defiance. Do not worry about the people who defy [God]. (5:68)*

Imagine, this system ('the *dīn* of the Truth') inaugurated by the blessed Prophet, which is 'Islam' or his 'form' of *islām*, was so broad that it permitted the People of the Book to practice and live their lives according to the Torah and Gospel. It extended the potential of salvation to members of all monotheistic religions thereby approving the plurality of religious devotions, expressions, cultures, and regulations.

Therefore, the *dīn* of the blessed Prophet gives a spiritual identity to Muslims by instituting devotional practices for them to adhere to; it acknowledges and respects the devotional practices and spiritual identities of members of other religions; and it provided generic regulations for the diverse human community of seventh century Medina. In other words, the blessed Prophet's expression of 'the *dīn* of Allah' gives the Muslim his identity and instructs him to pray towards the Ka'ba, and it also acknowledges the value of the rituals and devotions of other religions, such as the Jewish pilgrimage to the Holy Wall and the Hindu pilgrimage to the Ganges. Hence, it encourages Jews and Hindus to continue practicing Judaism and Hinduism respectively, reminding them of the 'essence' of their respective religions, which is God-centricity.

Consider the following verse again:

We have revealed to you [O Muhammad of] the Book with the truth, as a confirmation of what came before It of the Book, and as a sure witness over it. So judge between them according to what Allah has revealed, and do not follow their whims instead of what has come to you of the truth. We have assigned a law and a path to each of you. If Allah willed, He would have made you one people, but He wanted to test you in what He has given you. So compete [with each other] in good deeds; your return, all of you, is to Allah; and He will inform you of what you used to differ about. (5:48)

The tone of this verse, and others like it, makes it clear that the plurality and diversity of religions is *divinely decreed*. Allah is saying: 'Had I wanted, I would have made you into one people, but I will not make you into one people.' (5:48) Now think about this very carefully: Had God made us all the same, this world would never have evolved and progressed. You need diverse perspectives from different regions of the world at various times to bring about that contrast and greater charm. Black and white are necessary to figure out that humanity is beyond colour distinction. Male and female are necessary for people to realise that spiritual goodness transcends gender. The phenomena of rich and poor, and sick and healthy, are necessary to bring about that commonality within humankind. We need one person to say, 'I see it in *this* way', and another person to say, 'No, I see it in *that* way'. We need to look at both perspectives to see if they can yield a greater truth – a synthesis. The whole charm of life is in its plurality. In fact, plurality is the 'essence' of human growth, for without plurality, humankind cannot grow. We all have different perspectives: when we share, we grow.

Every faith oriented towards a virtuous God has the potential to guide its members to actualise their godly potential. Each provides its members with a theology to be internalised, and devotional and societal regulations to be adhered to. A completely accurate appreciation of the Unity of God is not 'essential' for salvation; hence, partially inaccurate conceptions of the Unity of God do not necessarily impede salvation. What is 'essential' for salvation is the subjective component of inner surrender to God. Ultimately, it is the type and degree of inner orientation to God that determines the path of human actualisation we take. Orientation to a virtuous God causes virtues and God-centricity to emerge in us, whereas an orientation towards evil and opposition to God results in us accruing vices and being egocentric. Basically, there are two paths: the path of God and the path of the ego, or in other words the path of 'the friends of God' and the path of 'the enemies of God'. All religions or ways of life (*adyān*) are built on one of these the two '*milla*' (or archetypical religions).

The people of Mecca wrote to the Prophet requesting amnesty as *kuffār* (disbelievers). When the Prophet refused, they claimed unfair treatment on the grounds that the Zoroastrians were allowed to practice their faith and were given the status of 'the People of the Book' despite being ditheistic (that is, believing in two divine agencies in addition to the one Supreme Being) and having norms and practices significantly different to those of the Abrahamic faiths. The Prophet replied that the Zoroastrians had received a divine Book and prophets; they were monotheistic 'in essence' despite their worship of the stars. Hence, the Prophet tolerated the Zoroastrians' wayward notions of God because their theology advocated servitude and surrender to the same God 'essentially'. Now the Meccans could have responded that they too were monotheistic 'in essence'; however, they did not. Their problem was with God Himself. They preferred to continue worshiping gods that ordained indecencies, injustices, exploitation, and oppression. The blessed Prophet could never tolerate this, and so he did not agree to their requests. They eventually gave up their faith and accepted Islam. Upon their conversion, the prophecy in the verse "He it is Who sent His Messenger with guidance and 'the religion of the Truth', that He might cause it to prevail over all religions..." (9:33) was realised. The blessed Prophet had established his 'form' of *islām* (or 'the *dīn* of Allah') throughout the region by the end of his life. It subsumed every possible faith, religion, sect, or way of life that was God-centric. Hence, it was the first and last religion to explicitly acknowledge the existential fact of the variety and plurality of religions.

Lecture Seven

Quran as a Contextual Expression of the Book

In this lecture, we will focus on the Holy Quran. We Muslims have certain assumptions about the Quran that need to be examined. There is no doubt that the Quran is a miracle in terms of its nature and function. It is unequalled in its content, eloquence, and consistency leaving no doubt as to its divine origin. However, we encounter several major problems due to our assumptions of what the 'miraculous nature' of the Quran means. The most pressing of them is the assumption of the immutability of the regulations of the Quran and the ensuing inconsistency between this assumption and the fact that the human condition is ever evolving. Let us explain this in clearer terms.

The Quran is the final communication from the divine source, and therefore we assume that it is as eternal as the Source from whence it has come. The implication of this is that we assume it is all inclusive and its regulations are universally applicable to all regions of every era. Additionally, the status of sanctity conferred upon the Quran by the Muslim mind has resulted in its ceremonialisation – the practice of ritually reciting the Quran in Arabic, without understanding its content, for the purpose of gaining rewards in the month of Ramadan and so on.

The impact of such a sacrosanct status of the Quran is as follows: Firstly, it dissuades us from critically examining the contents of the Quran to personally ascertain its validity, which contravenes the instruction of the Quran itself to examine its content critically; in fact, the contrary occurs – I feel forced to verify its content as a matter of faith without any prior critical engagement with it. Secondly, since the 'sacrosanct-ness' of the Quran is extended to each of its letters, every verse is held in equal esteem. Thirdly, its devotional and societal regulations are believed to be both immutable and optimal for bringing about the most effective and productive life due to the assumption of the eternality of its verses. Finally, we believe the Quran contains all future knowledge based on our assumption of its comprehensiveness. Accordingly, the solutions to all problems, including future ones, must be sourced from it either directly or indirectly.

I repeat: There is no doubt as to the divine origins of the Quran and its sacrosanct status, eternality, universality, finality, and comprehensiveness. However, these properties of the Quran are true of its 'essence' and not its 'form'. Problems arise when the properties of 'finality' and 'universality' are assigned to the literal word of the Quran as opposed to its meaning, especially in the domain of its regulations. We will cite examples of the problems created by designating 'sacredness' and 'immutability' to its literal word as opposed to its meaning. Initially, we will examine problems arising from our assumptions generally before tackling the issue of the Sharia regulations of the Quran. We will demonstrate that no such contention exists between these properties of the Quran and its content when viewed in light of the notions of 'form' and 'essence'.

Think about these assumptions carefully: If the regulations of the Quran are applicable till the Day of Qiyāma in the simplistic manner in which we have understood (which includes its formulation of rights and societal regulations), then obviously 'beating wives', 'cutting hands', 'possessing slaves', and 'taking concubines' are not only acceptable, but they constitute the optimal system of rights and regulations for all of time, including today. The justification for this is that the text is from God, and so it is sacred, 'final', and hence immutable. Now does our intuition agree to such a system of rights and regulations at present? Would we be able to justify them rationally? Would not advocating such regulations create an internal conflict within our minds and be a cause for embarrassment? If the answer to this last question is 'yes', then how can anything from God be a cause for internal conflict or embarrassment?

During my *tafsīr* sessions on Sūra al-Zumar, I asked the attendees about the following verse, "And certainly We have coined for humankind in this Quran every example..." (39:27): 'Does that mean God has supplied us with every example in the Quran?' They replied: 'Yes.' I asked: 'Where is the example of the *crocodile* and *jungle*?'

What does it mean by 'every example'? There is a lot of naïveté, laziness, and lack of responsible thinking in the way we assume things. Are we not assuming a little too much? Think about it: The Quran states to its initial audience that 'We have provided you with every example', but they did not interject and say that that was not true – that not *every* example is given. Does this not demonstrate that the Quran is using language in a particular manner which the people were accustomed to? Thus, when it says that it has given 'every example', it can only mean that it has given enough pertinent examples related to the theme it is conveying. It does not mean 'every example' per se.

Fazlur Rahman (d. 1988) addresses the notion of the eternality of the regulations of the Quran. He observes that to keep the verses that prescribe fighting with 'the enemies of God' eternally active and relevant, we will be compelled to create 'the enemies of God' in every generation in order to fight them. Similarly with the slavery and concubinage regulations in the Sharia, we will always have to conquer lands and take slaves in order to own slaves and have concubines, just to ensure the regulations of the Quran remain eternal.

The assumption of the 'sacredness' of the Arabic language emerged as a result of it being the language of the Quran. Obviously, the language of the text of the Quran is merely a 'formalistic' feature of the divine revelation. It is not an 'essential' feature of the Quran as a 'source of guidance' per se. 'The Book' from which the Quran originates is beyond language, and It is the source of all the other revelations which were revealed to people with different languages. The Muslim community is obliged to believe in the content of the Old Testament and Gospel, both of which were conveyed in languages other than Arabic. In fact, the Quran asserts that all revelations convey the same 'essential' message as itself despite being in different languages. Therefore, the Arabic language is a 'formalistic' feature of the Quran. 'In essence', it has nothing to do with the Quran. Do not misunderstand me, I think Arabic is the best language. Even so, it is not an 'essential' feature of the Quran, the Book, or the Truth.

The assumption that all the verses of the Quran have the same profundity in meaning is unjustified. It is one thing to maintain that the Quran as a whole is unrivalled in its content, and another thing altogether to state that every part of it has the same depth of meaning as every other part. The Quran itself distinguishes verses that are 'firm' (meaning unambiguous and clear), which it terms as 'the Mother of the Book', from others that are 'ambiguous' (3:7). Note that the phrase 'the Mother of the Book' in this verse means 'the core verses the Quran'. So even God distinguishes the verses of the Quran in terms of degree and type of meaning.

Think about it: How can the verse *"tabbat yadā abī lahab wa-tabb"* ("May the hands of Abu Lahab perish, and may he perish [too]!", 111:1) be said to have the same profundity in meaning as the *basmala* ("In the name of Allah, the Most Compassionate, the Most Merciful")? How can they be said to have the same depth of meaning? Undoubtedly, they are the same insofar as they both come from God and are ordained by Him to be part of His Scripture, but how can they be said to have the same depth of meaning? Look at this phenomenal verse: "He is the First, the Last, the Outer, and the Inner; and He has knowledge of all things." (57:3). Now compare it with the following verse: "…so when Zayd had accomplished [his desire] from her [which was to divorce her] …" (33:37) How can these two verses be said to have the same profundity in meaning? Yes, they are the same insofar as they have both been revealed and ordained as revelation, but they do not have the same depth of meaning. We need to recheck such assumptions about the Quran. If we do, then our understanding of what the Quran is trying to convey will be far greater.

I always say that Sūra al-Qiyāma is very eloquent. People respond: 'How can you single it out as an eloquent *sūra*? Aren't all the *suras* equally eloquent?' Obviously, some are more eloquent than others. Similarly, some chapters (*sūras*) of the Quran are more integral to the message of God, or more 'essence-based', than others. Why is Sūra al-Fātiḥa called 'the Mother of the Quran'? If all the *suras* are the same, then why give preference to Sūra al-Fātiḥa over the others? Why is the Sūra al-Yāsīn designated as 'the Heart of the Quran'? If all the chapters were of equal significance in meaning, then why is the worth of a single recitation of Sūra al-Aḥad (*Qul Huwa Allah…*) equivalent to a third of the whole Quran? Why doesn't Sūra al-Kawthar (*Innā aʿṭaynāka al-Kawthar*) have the same worth? The blessed Prophet was very grateful that Sūra al-Fātiḥa (or *al-sabʿa al-mathānī* – the seven oft-repeated verses) was only revealed to him, for it is the greatest *sūra* to be revealed. Therefore, all the chapters (*sūras*) and verses of the Quran do not have the same depth of meaning. So, if one were to say that they find a particular *sūra's* eloquence to be phenomenal, it does not discredit the Quran in any way whatsoever. It is one thing to say that the whole Quran is unmatched in its eloquence, and another thing to say every verse is equally eloquent.

The notion of the 'sacredness' of the Quran has been a stumbling block for the Muslim community because we have not understood the meaning of 'sacred': We can declare something as 'sacred', but we also need to understand the meaning of 'sacred'. We can assert that something is 'sacred' because it is from God, but we also need to understand that everything is from God, and everything is transient. If the nature of everything in this world is transient, then how can something 'sacred' that is also from God be contrary to the nature of the rest of the world? If humankind is a transient reality – that is, since it is always flowing, fluid, on the move, and evolving – then how can the communication of God be stagnant? In fact, we know it has never been stagnant. The fact that God has communicated with us numerous times, in the 'forms' of the Scriptures of Ibrahim, the Torah, the Gospel, and the Quran, is itself evidence that His communication has undergone change and hence is in sync with the nature of this worldly existence. Every communication has been slightly different to the others. The same Book has been fashioned in three different ways within the Abrahamic faiths: The 'essence' of all three is the same despite their 'forms' being different. The Quran has an 'essence', which is 'the salient *milla* of Ibrahim', and it has a 'form' primarily addressing the human existential context of the blessed Prophet in which it was revealed. The same is true of the Scriptures of Ibrahim, the Torah, and the Gospel: they all share the same 'essence' as the Quran but differ in their 'forms' due to the different human existential contexts in which they were revealed.

The following verses illustrate these points. The Quran makes a sharp distinction between the Quran and '*al-Kitāb*':

> *He has the keys to the unseen; none knows them but Him. He knows all that is in the land and sea. No leaf falls but He knows it, nor is there a single grain in the darkness of the earth, nor anything fresh or withered, but it is in a Clear Book. (6:59)*

The verse does not state that the Quran contains the details of all things; it asserts that all such details are in *al-Kitāb al-Mubīn* (the Clear Book). Think about this carefully. "Allah effaces whatever He wants, and He establishes [whatever He wants]; and with Him is the Mother of the Book." (13:39) What is '*Umm al-Kitāb*', 'the Mother of the Book'? In the following verse, Allah introduces the notion of 'a Protected Record' (*lawḥ maḥfūz*): "Indeed, it is the Majestic Quran in a Protected Record." (85:21-2) What is this 'Protected Record'? Finally, Allah makes a distinction between the Quran and 'a Hidden Book' (*Kitāb Maknūn*): "Indeed, it is the Noble Quran in a Hidden Book; none touches it save the purified ones." (56:77-79) How is it even possible for anyone to touch this 'Book' when it is 'hidden'? Allama Tabataba'i states that the expression 'the purified ones' (*al-muṭahharūn*) refers to those who have attained the purity of the Intellect (or Heart) whereby they have recourse to 'the Real Book' by means of contemplating the Quran.

Thus, Allah distinguishes between the Quran and 'the Book'. Consider the following verse: "Our Lord, and raise up in their midst a messenger from among them who shall recite to them Your communications and teach them the Book and the Wisdom, and purify them..." (2:129) Here, Ibrahim prays to Allah to send a messenger to a future people who will teach them 'the Book' in addition to reciting the verses of His communication (that is, the Quran). Thus, in the mind of Prophet Ibrahim, there is a difference between 'revelation' and 'the Book'. Similarly, Allah says regarding the Prophets Musa and Isa: "And We gave the Book and *al-Furqān* (the Distinguisher) to Musa." (2:53) and "He will teach him (Isa) the Book and Wisdom, and the Torah and the Gospel." (3:48) Therefore, there is a distinction between 'the Book' and the Quran, the Torah and the Gospel. Finally, consider the following verse: "We have revealed to you the Book with truth as a confirmation of what was before it (that is, the Torah and the Gospel) ...". (5:48 and 3:3) Again, this verse makes it clear that 'the Book' is different from the Torah and Gospel and yet connected with them. Therefore, we conclude that there is a distinction between 'the Book' and the Quran, 'the Book' and the Torah, and 'the Book' and the Gospel; the Quran, Torah and Gospel are expressions or 'forms' of 'the Book' and not 'the Book' per se.

It should be noted that the meaning of the word *dhālika* in the following verse of the Quran is 'that', but it can also be used to signify 'this' semantically: "That Book (*dhālik al-kitāb*) in which there is no doubt." (2:2) This is the first verse to be revealed in Medina after the Prophet's migration; hence, it marks the beginning of the revelation of the largest chapters (*sūras*) of the Quran, such as *al-Baqara, Āl-Imrān*, and *al-Nisā'*, which include the majority of the *ahkām* (devotional and societal regulations) of Islam. Thus, when Allah says "*dhālik al-kitāb*" in this verse (2:2), it means *that* Book. Of course, it is legitimate to take it to mean 'this book' in the sense of the Quran that is in the process of being revealed; however, it must be accompanied with the understanding that the Quran is nothing other than 'the Book' being conveyed in the Prophet's context.

Now consider the following verse:

> *Say [O believers], 'We [Muslims] believe in Allah and what has been revealed to us and what was revealed to Ibrahim, Ismail, Ishaq, Yaqub, and the Tribes, and [we believe in] what was given to Musa and Isa, and what was given to the prophets from their Lord; we do not make any distinction between any of them (prophets), and we surrender to Him. (2:136)*

The implication here is that whatever was revealed previously and whatever has been revealed to the Prophet and the Muslims is one and the same thing. Obviously, they are different revelations, and yet we are commanded to believe in all of them equally. If they were mutually inconsistent with each other, God cannot ask us to believe in all of them; hence, there has to be consistency. Based on our preceding deliberations, 'the Book' is an overwhelming reality being revealed from time to time in different expressions: At one particular time and place, it expresses itself as the Scripture of Musa, at another time and place, as the Scripture of Isa, and then as the Scripture of the blessed Prophet Muhammad in seventh century Arabia. It is the same truth and reality being sent time and again in differing circumstances, and hence It has expressed Itself in the respective languages and idioms of the different contexts in which It was revealed. In other words, all the revelations retain 'the essence' of 'the Book' despite the differences of language, idioms, examples, norms, and regulations between them.

For greater clarity, consider the following verses in Sūra al-Zumar, "The [gradual] revelation of the Book is from Allah, the Mighty, the Wise. Surely, We have [completely] revealed to you the Book with the truth; therefore, serve Allah, being sincere to Him in the religion (*dīn*)." (39:1-2) 'The Book' is mentioned twice in these two verses, one after another. Obviously, God does not say anything in vain, and so He does not repeat unnecessarily. The verbal noun *tanzīl* is used regarding 'the Book' in the first instance, and a verb of the verbal noun *inzāl* is employed in the second instance, again regarding 'the Book'. Upon analysis of their morphology (verbal forms) and semantics, scholars have said that *tanzīl* denotes 'sequential revelation', and *inzāl* and its verbs imply 'the instantaneous experience of the entirety of revelation'. Therefore, God is asserting that 'the Book' has been delivered in both ways: sequentially and gradually (*tanzīlī*), and instantaneously and completely (*inzālī*). Thus, 'the Book' has been revealed gradually, and it has been revealed instantaneously in its entirety. For instance, the verse "Indeed, We revealed it [completely and instantaneously] during the Night of Grandeur" (97:1) means that the entirety of the Quran was revealed during that Night instantaneously. The verb '*anzalnā*', which is a verb of the verbal noun *inzāl*, is employed in this verse. In contrast, we know that all the verses of the Quran were occasioned by contextual demands (*sha'n al-nuzūl*), that is, they were revealed gradually and sequentially in response to contextual situations, that is, as and when the need arose.

Therefore, 'the Book' is an overwhelming existential reality, revealed from time to time via successive messengers to their respective communities. The process of revelation consists of two steps: First, the Scripture, such as the Quran, is revealed instantaneously in its entirety to a certain plane or realm of communication. Second, the Scripture is conveyed gradually from that plane or realm of communication to a prophet, such as the blessed Prophet, throughout his mission as and when it (the Scripture) is occasioned by events and circumstances.

Consider the following verses: "*Ha Mim*. By the Clear Book. Indeed, We have made It an Arabic Quran that you may understand. And surely It is in 'the Mother of the Book' with Us, truly elevated, full of wisdom." (43:1-4) Thus, 'the Arabic Quran' is a rendering of 'the Clear Book' which is contained within 'the Mother of the Book'. The notion of 'the Arabic Quran' being a 'form' of 'the Clear Book' is also mentioned in the following verses: "*Alif Lam Ra*. These are the verses of the Clear Book. Indeed, We have revealed it as an Arabic Quran that you may understand." (12:1-2) Thus, Allah has revealed *al-Kitāb al-Mubīn* (the Clear Book), which is within 'the Mother of the Book', as an "Arabic Quran". Regarding 'the Clear Book', the Quran states, "... He knows all that is in the land and sea. No leaf falls but He knows it, nor is there a single grain in the darkness of the earth, nor anything fresh or withered, but it is in a Clear Book." (6:59); and with respect to 'the Mother of the Book', Allah states that He "effaces whatever He wants, and He establishes [whatever He wants]; and with Him is 'the Mother of the Book.'" (13:39)

Based on the above references and deliberations, we begin to understand that these notions are references to grand existential realities: 'The Mother of Book' is the Ultimate Reality with

God. 'The Clear Book' is also an eternal and universal Reality and Truth for it is a part of 'the Mother of Book'. It contains the details of all affairs in their entirety: "No affliction befalls in the earth or in yourselves, but it is in a Book, before We bring it about; indeed, that is easy for Allah." (57:22) Lastly, 'the Arabic Quran' is a contextual 'form' of 'the Clear Book'.

Therefore, the Quran is 'sacred' insofar as it is a revelation from the divine source. This is the meaning of its 'sacredness'. Hence, there is no 'sacredness' regarding its face-value appreciation, by which we mean its 'conventional linguistic meaning'. The problems of the 'sacrosanct-ness' of the Quran (mentioned at the beginning of this lecture) stem from the understanding that the Eternal Source knows what is best for us and has spoken in a clear language. It is assumed that the face-value appreciation of its legal verses reveals their meanings as 'intended by God'. Consequently, a sacrosanct status is conferred upon 'the face-value appreciation' as the method for interpreting its legal verses, for it yields regulations 'intended by Him' assumed to be for all times, places, and peoples. Hence, 'the face-value appreciation' cannot be challenged as a method of interpretation according to scholars.

There is no doubt that 'the face-value appreciation' of the legal verses of the Quran does yield the 'forms' of regulations 'intended by God', but only for the people of the context in which they were revealed, namely the Muslims of seventh century Arabia. To assume it ('the face-value appreciation') reveals the 'forms' of regulations 'intended by God' for people of every context, that is, for people of all times and places, results in the universalisation of what is essentially contextual (that is, the 'form' of regulations) and the disregarding of the changing temporal human context during the process of deriving regulations.

In actual fact, God never even intended for the initial audience to perform the 'forms' of the regulations *per se*, let alone subsequent Muslims; rather, the performance of their 'forms' was always for the purpose of attaining their 'essences'. In other words, God's intention is that humans, irrespective of time and place, attain the 'essences' of regulations, for they are eternal, immutable, and universal. Thus, if the performance of the 'form' of the regulation does not result in the attainment of its 'essence', then the 'form' of the regulation needs modification. This means we need to know the sacred 'essences' of the regulations so that we are able to fashion them into befitting 'forms' for newer contexts. The method of knowing the sacred 'essences' includes the face-value appreciation of the legal verses among other things.

Consider the following (which is based on a chronological reading of revelation): Initially in Mecca, most of the revelation consisted of the 'essential' teachings, that is, it conveyed the necessity of godliness, the belief in the Hereafter, and the performance of charitable acts. When the numbers of followers of the Prophet increased such that they could be classified as a very small community, these 'essential' teachings acquired appropriate 'forms' in the domains of devotional and societal regulations; however, they were very few and simple. Then when Prophet Muhammad and his followers migrated to Medina, many more 'forms' were instituted, and in certain cases previous 'forms' were abrogated and replaced by newer 'forms', which is attested to and evident in the Quran itself. This change in the numbers and complexity of the 'forms' of regulations was due to the 'growth' of the Muslim community as per 'the existential property of growth'.

This evolution in the 'form' of a regulation is evident in the major devotional rituals of ṣalāt and zakāt, both of which have gone through significant 'formal' modifications during the Prophet's mission. Their 'forms' in the initial Meccan period were very different to their 'forms' in the latter Meccan period, which in turn were very different to their 'forms' in Medina. However, their 'essences' remained the same throughout all their 'formal' modifications, for the 'essences' are the desired objectives or 'intentions' of God behind His command to perform them. Similarly, societal rules fluctuated according to the demands of the context (the time, place, and people); for instance, soon after his arrival in Medina, the blessed Prophet legislated mutual inheritance between a Muslim resident of Medina and a Muslim migrant by virtue of the official but arbitrary bond of brotherhood between them that he had instituted earlier. This regulation was abrogated later in the Medinan period.

The 'essence' governing all societal regulations and conferring upon them the status of 'regulations as intended by God' is 'the principle of justice' as understood by the degree of growth of 'human nobility' of the collectivity in any given time and place, which is attested to by the Quran and human reason. The application of 'the principle of justice' in light of 'human nobility' results in different 'forms' of societal regulations. In other words, when jurists of collectivities with differing degrees of 'human nobility' apply 'the principle of justice' during their derivations of societal regulations, the 'forms' of regulations will be different for each collectivity. This is the reason why we find different societal regulations on the same issue in different contexts, for instance, the regulation on the punishment for a thief.

Thus, the 'forms' of the societal regulations in the Quran are not eternal or uniform, nor can they be universally applicable to every time and place, due to the relativistic nature of 'human nobility' from one region to another. The relativity of 'human nobility' is the result of different degrees of rational, moral, and spiritual growth of different collectives. This will also be discussed in greater detail in due course.

It should be noted that 'the face-value appreciation' of the Quran's discourse on the nature of God, God-human relations, God-centricity, human psychology, 'the righteous deed', the Day of Qiyāma, and reward and punishment, are eternal. This is because these issues are not contextual (that is, they are not only true for people of a particular time and place), but rather they are universal (that is, they are true for people of all times and places).

Verses of the Quran alluding to the observable cosmos and natural phenomena, such as the creation of the heavens and earth, the expansion of heaven, and embryology, often include explanations of the 'seen' aspects of the natural world and cosmos, which are scientific issues in and of themselves. As such, the content of such verses cannot be described as 'truths' or 'statements of fact' about the 'seen' aspects of the natural world and cosmos, for their meanings are ambiguous. This ambiguity is due to the limitations of the language of the time insofar as it lacked the precise vocabulary to express such truths clearly. Despite this, all such verses are *pointing* to 'truths' or 'facts' about the 'seen' aspects of the natural world and cosmos, and hence they are not open to revision. In fact, they will be understood better as our understanding of the 'seen' aspects of the natural world and cosmos increase.

Another set of verses of the Quran recount historical events. These are facts about the past and so can never be subject to change. They describe particular moments in time and space and hence are not 'universal' statements in and of themselves; however, the ethos and moral lessons contained within them are 'universal'. This is also true of the personal circumstances of the blessed Prophet alluded to in the Quran. For instance, there are verses addressing the anxiety he experienced at certain points during his mission, others focus on his interactions with his wives and the norms instituted for them specifically, and a few verses mention his dealings with specific people, such as Abu Lahab and Zayd (the uncle and adopted son of the Prophet respectively). Such verses also cannot be described as 'eternal' or 'universal' in and of themselves for they describe particular moments of history; however, the ethos and moral lessons contained within them are 'universal'.

Regarding the Quran's devotional and societal regulations, we know that the 'essences' of all regulations are eternal, universal and immutable, and not their 'forms'. That being said, the 'forms' of devotional regulations are pretty much immutable and universal, meaning that only very few and slight modifications to their 'forms' are possible. This is because we are bound to this worldly terrestrial existence which does not undergo changes to the degree that would warrant drastic 'formal' changes to them. However, should some of us move away from the earth or if there are drastic changes affecting the way we live on earth, then the 'forms' of devotional regulations will require modification to remain optimal in facilitating the growth of the individual and collectivity. In contrast to devotional regulations, societal regulations undergo continuous modifications, additions, and abrogations due to the constantly fluctuating societal context and natural world, and the ever-evolving nature of the individual's and collectivity's rationality, morality, and spirituality.

I recall the late Imam Khomeini (d. 1989) stating in his sermons that the Quran has been watered down seventy times before it reached us. In other words, 'the Book' has been diluted seventy times prior to it being revealed in the 'form' of the Quran. The Quran was revealed in the language of the people of a particular time and place, during particular circumstances – all of which are limitations upon 'the Book'. The Arabic language, as eloquent as it is, is a limitation upon the 'essence' that the Quran is conveying. This is because it (the Arabic language) can only facilitate the communication of the 'essence' within the limits and flexibility of its notions and concepts, and the limits of the knowledge base of the people. The Quran could not have cited the example of 'spaceships' for instance to explain its points because the people of the seventh century did not have the knowledge of such a concept. Yet the Quran had to be revealed to them, and so they were made to understand it by means of the language they spoke and the examples they could relate to. Thus, the Quran was bound by the language of its immediate audience and the examples they could make sense of. For instance, the Quran uses the example of the camel as opposed to the sloth to make its point in the following verse: "Do they not consider the camels, how they were created?" (88:17)

We know that the *sharia* regulations of 'the *dīn* of Allah' have undergone numerous modifications between the eras of the Prophets Nuh and Muhammad, and that this was in response to 'the existential property of growth' causing changes in the rational, moral, and spiritual aspects of the human individual and collectivity. To assert that there cannot be any more changes to the Sharia regulations till the Day of Qiyāma is to declare that the steady growth of the human community resulting from 'the existential property of growth' has ceased. Is it not absurd to claim that human beings have stopped growing after Prophet Muhammad? Has the human community not grown after the revelatory era? Undoubtedly it has. In fact, its rate of growth in the last two centuries has been faster than all preceding eras of human history to the best of our knowledge. Therefore, how can the renewal of the Sharia, which we have substantiated as having historical precedence, come to a halt? The root of the problem here is our naïve assumption of 'the finality' of the literal word.

I once said to a very learned man: 'A fast cannot be twenty or twenty-two hours in summer and four or six hours in winter just because the text defines the "the day" as beginning at sunrise and ending at sunset. The duration of the fast must be for a period of time that is reasonable and beneficial. Accordingly, a fast may end prior to sunset or after it, depending on where you are in the world and what season it is.' He replied: 'That is counter-intuitive.' I said: 'Surely fasting for more than twenty or less than six hours a day for thirty days consecutively is counter-intuitive. The problem is that since we Muslims have believed that sunrise and sunset are the markers for the beginning and end of the day since childhood, a strong association has formed between them in our minds and so we will apply them irrespective of where we are in the world, even if the duration between them is two hours.'

Often counter-intuitive practices become so familiar, habitual, and embedded in our minds over time that 'intuitive' practices contravening them are not seen as such and are in fact thought of as 'counter-intuitive'. Imagine if the earth's axial rotation slowed down resulting in alternating periods of light and dark, each lasting forty hours (which is actually foretold in our eschatological literature), will we fast for forty hours straight followed by forty hours of rest?

We have to appreciate that prior to the revelation of the Quran, the Arabs were demarcating 'daytime' in terms of sunrise and sunset, and dividing the day according to certain positions of the sun in the sky, and that these were the only means of defining the 'day', measuring time, and dividing the 'conventional' day available to them. Subsequently, the Quran obliged fasting during the days of the month of Ramadhan, and it defined the 'conventional' day as beginning at sunrise and ending at sunset. With time, the duration of the fast became associated with sunrise and sunset in the minds of the people and the notion of fasting for the duration of the 'conventional' day was forgotten.

The Quran was the primary source of guidance for its immediate audience, and as such, it had to be pragmatic, which means it had to comply with their immediate context. The revelation took the strengths and weaknesses of its audience and their contexts into account and then formulated itself accordingly. Its task was to provide its initial audience with an appropriate 'form' of a just, virtuous, and progressive social system with an in-built potential and flexibility for reformulation. Of course, the Quran does this – it fashions 'just' regulations indicating the potential for reformulation – with regards to both its devotional and societal regulations. For instance, the Quran used every opportunity to establish the practice of freeing a slave as one of the options of the compensatory regulation (*kaffāra*) and as a highly rewardable practice in and of itself, thereby instilling the notion of the necessity to emancipate slaves within the hearts and minds of the people. Such instructions were intended to be an initial step towards the diffusion and recognition of the notion of human dignity in society with the hope that human minds would abolish slavery altogether in due course.

Consider the verse instructing the presence of two female witnesses during the witness-testimony of a woman, as opposed to a single male witness if the testifier is a man. The verse indicates the 'core value' or 'essence' of the formulation by offering the rationale behind the requirement of the presence of two women as opposed to just one: "… so that if one of the two [women] errs, the other will remind her…" (2:282). Therefore, the 'core value' or 'essence' in such regulations is 'ensuring accurate testimony'. Accordingly, regulations instructing the presence of two female witnesses on the basis that memory lapses are more common among women than men must be revised in eras and regions in which women are accustomed to retaining information as accurately as men.

The verse of the Quran expressing the superiority of husbands over their wives states the 'core reason' for this disparity as 'grace from God and the norm (which was prevalent at the time) of men utilising their wealth for the upkeep of their families' (the implication being that women did not utilise their wealth as such): "Men are the maintainers of women because Allah has made some of them to excel others and because they spend out of their property…" (4:34). Imagine a future world in which the modes of trade and warfare change from physical exertion to mental activity and women are more accomplished in these jobs than men, then the situation will be reversed: wives will be superior to their husbands due to the grace of God and because they utilise more of their wealth than their husbands for the upkeep of their families. Similar analyses hold true for the laws of inheritance, severing of limbs, public floggings, the notion of interest, and inter-human relations: all such regulations and norms have 'essences' or 'values' that are universal and in need of reformulation in differing contexts.

Fundamentally, the human condition is one of growth and evolution, and so the main value or 'essence' driving the revelation of societal regulations is 'the progression of humankind'.

Hence, regulations were formulated in light of this value (that is, 'the progression of humankind'), 'the principle of justice' and 'human nobility'. In fact, even regulations pertaining to devotional acts are subject to fluctuations in order to safe-guard and secure this central value (of 'the progression of humankind') and their own particular values or 'essences'. The difference between the devotional and societal regulations is that the formulation of devotional regulations is totally dependent upon Sharia texts. In other words, revelation's role in formulating devotional regulations is 'essential' and 'innovative' because the human mind is incapable of fashioning their 'essences' into optimal 'forms' independently of it. Hence, they are subject to minimal modifications. Their 'forms' have the dual purpose of securing their 'essence', which is God-centricity, and giving us our religious identity.

In contrast, societal regulations, including socio-economic systems, belong to the domain of humankind 'in essence' and are fully subject to the state of flux. Their formulation is on-going, and they can be, have been, and are meant to be formulated by human reason. This means revelation's role in formulating societal regulations, including socio-economic systems and the system of human rights, is 'accidental' or 'non-essential'. In other words, its 'essence' or main purpose is not to formulate societal regulations. When it does formulate them, it is merely aiding human reason and is corroborative of it. This is because all societal regulations, including those formulated by revelation, are beholden to existential values and dynamism, as will be explained in due course. To reiterate, whenever revelation has issued societal regulations, it has done so in the capacity of human reason and merely supplied befitting 'forms' for the people of the context it was addressing by assessing their rational, moral, and spiritual needs accurately.

Throughout these lectures, we have stated that the outward expression of *islām* or 'the *dīn* of Allah' has been changing constantly in terms of its 'forms'. These 'forms' have been conveyed by successive revelations. The fact that subsequent revelations either replaced or modified the societal regulations of previous ones shows that 'the literal word' of revelation (and its face-value appreciation) does not have 'sacredness' or 'finality' as such. The fact that the Quran acknowledges the process of abrogation regarding its own regulations demonstrates that the value of regulations is not in the 'form' per se, but rather it is in the purpose the 'form' serves. It should be noted that the ultimate purpose of both devotional and societal regulations is to create a virtuous and godly collectivity.

The plurality and diversity of devotional regulations among the different religions and their respective sects is sanctioned by the Quran because they all retain the 'essence', which is God-centricity. Their origins are their respective revelations and hence changes to them have been minimal historically. In contrast, societal regulations need constant monitoring and tweaking because their subject matter, which is human actions and interactions, is in a constant state of flux due to the dynamic nature of existence in general. The process of constantly monitoring and tweaking ensures they continue to be optimal in facilitating the rational, moral, and spiritual growth of humans whose 'aptitudes' (that is, psychological, cognitive, and moral aptitudes), circumstances, and societal set-ups are continually changing.

In conclusion, societal regulations are not an 'essential' part of religion. They have been and continue to be formulated by human reason independently of revelation in light of morality with the view to contributing to 'the optimal and most productive way of life' for the individual and collectivity. They are formulated to regulate all aspects of societal life, such as the economy, politics, and human and animal welfare. Thus, societal regulations contained within the Quran are to be considered as 'non-essential', rational, and moral formulations supplied by the revelation to a particular time and place based on 'the existential property of growth' (or in other words, with a view to contributing to 'the optimal and most productive way of life').

This means societal regulations are not a divine and an inviolable aspect of religious teachings, and it is wrong to view them as such. Revelation supplied these regulations in accordance with the pre-existing aptitudes, circumstances, and societal set-ups of its audience in order to facilitate their growth. The proof of their being rational 'essentially' is that they were embraced by the community on the basis that they made sense and were fair and productive. In other words, the audience was able to affirm their content and worth and accept them readily because they were rational and moral at the time of revelation.

Just as the omission of the draconian punishment of stoning to death from the Quran is indicative of the collectivity having evolved from the time of Prophet Musa up to Prophet Muhammad, similarly the collectivity has continued to grow from the era of the Quranic revelation up to the present. Human aptitudes, nobility, and dignity have evolved and consequently need to be reflected in societal regulations and the formulation of rights.

Finally, the formulation of societal regulations is governed by 'the principle of justice' as appreciated by the degree of growth of 'human nobility' of the collectivity in any given time and place. In view of a continually changing context, ensuring that regulations conform to 'the principle of justice' and 'human nobility' will of necessity result in a departure from 'the face-value appreciation' of the societal regulations in the Quran. This does not constitute a violation of the 'sacred' or 'divine' regulations because it is 'the principle of justice' understood in light of 'human nobility' that is the 'essence' of the societal regulations of the Quran. The phenomenon of abrogation in the Quran is itself a proof of the dynamism of society necessitating different formulations of 'the principle of justice' and 'human nobility': a norm that was 'just' and 'noble' yesterday is 'unjust' and 'ignoble' today. The fact that societal regulations of the new Sharia of Prophet Muhammad made more sense to the people than those of previous *sharias*, enabling them to challenge previous regulations on the basis of morality, demonstrates that they were rational and moral 'in essence', and hence were based on 'the principle of justice' and 'human nobility'.

It is said that when the Mahdi gains a following, he will be accused of changing the faith. Obviously, the Mahdi will not be instructing people to abandon God-centricity, nor will he ask them to stop praying and fasting. Recall that only societal regulations have the potential for change. Hence, the Mahdi will merely legislate new societal regulations for which he will be accused of changing the faith by scholars no less. Moreover, we can surmise that his legislating and instituting new societal regulations will be purpose-driven, that is, it will not be arbitrary and pointless. This means his reformulation of societal regulations will be governed by 'the existential property of growth', that is, with a view to contributing to 'the optimal and most productive way of life'; for he will view societal regulations as a means to creating a virtuous and godly collectivity, and not as an end in itself.

Lecture Eight
The Finality of the Sharia

A Muslim is one who subscribes to the 'finality' of the Sharia of Islam. The word 'Sharia' refers to the entirety of the teachings delivered by Prophet Muhammad. In the last lecture, we discussed how the assumption of the 'finality' of the Quran is problematic in the domain of Quranic regulations generally and societal ones in particular. However, the problem is not restricted to the regulations of the Quran but extends to the entirety of Sharia regulations, that is, 'finality' is believed to be true of the Sunna of the Prophet also. In the Twelver Shia faith, the notion of 'finality' is also applied to the legal teachings of the impeccable Imams. Their teachings are by far the largest and most relied upon source for the extrapolation of Sharia regulations in the Twelver Shia legal tradition. Thus, the problematisation of the assumption of 'finality' also has implications for our understanding of the significance of the teachings of the impeccable Imams.

Consider the following statement attributed to the sixth Imam: 'There is nothing a Muslim is in need of save it is contained within the Book and the Sunna.' 'The Book' refers to the Quran in the context of this narration. Similarly, consider the following report attributed to the sixth Imam: 'The permissible (*ḥalāl*) of Muhammad will remain permissible till the Day of Qiyāma, and the prohibited (*ḥarām*) of Muhammad will remain prohibited until the Day of Qiyāma.' The face-value understanding of such texts is that every possible Sharia regulation is in the Quran and Sunna, including those pertaining to newer situations, and so the faithful are required to merely consult these Sharia texts and locate the appropriate regulations.

Such texts must presuppose the dichotomy of the 'form' and 'essence' of a regulation (the 'form' being perfect in and for its own original context but not beyond it, and the 'essence' being 'universal' and 'eternal' and needing to be secured in every 'form'), for otherwise they do not make sense and are problematic. The regulations formulated at the time of the revelation were optimal in facilitating the rational, moral, and spiritual growth of the people of its context, just as Mosaic law was optimal for the people of its own context. However, neither are optimal beyond their own respective contexts, that is, for people belonging to different contexts. The 'values' or 'essences' contained within both the Mosaic law and Quranic regulations are 'eternal' and 'universal'. They remain true until 'the Day of Qiyāma'. Hence, it is these 'values' or 'essences' in the Quran and Sunna that are to be applied beyond their own respective contexts and refashioned into befitting 'forms' for differing contexts.

The fact that there are numerous differences between the regulations of the different *sharias* of the prophets is proof that modifying regulations into befitting 'forms' for different contexts was the norm historically: regulations of former *sharias* would be abrogated or modified by subsequent ones due to changes in the context. Obviously, the 'forms' of regulations of previous *sharias* would only be altered in later ones if the context had changed and the 'forms' were not optimal; hence, many 'forms' of regulations of previous *sharias* would not be altered in later ones if the context remained the same and the 'forms' were optimal. For instance, the law of retaliation – 'an eye for an eye' – was formulated prior to the *sharia* of Musa and was retained by the Quran, that is, it was not abrogated. Similarly, many of the laws of consumption in the previous *sharias*, such as the prohibition of consuming the flesh of swine, were not altered. In contrast, the law of stoning adulterers to death, which was part of the Jewish *sharia*, was abrogated by virtue of the Quran prescribing alternative 'forms' of punishment and omitting its mention as a 'form' altogether. The same phenomenon is observed in the Quran's abrogation of its own verses. Later verses modified and at times abrogated earlier ones because the 'forms' of regulations stated in earlier verses were no longer yielding the anticipated 'values' in different contexts; hence, there was a need for newer 'forms' of those same 'values', which were supplied in the later verses.

The predominant understanding of the aforementioned narrations is that 'the letter' of the law of the Quran and Sunna applies to the people of all times and places until the end of human existence on earth. This means that the assumptions of 'finality' and 'universality' apply not only to the Quran, but to the Sunna as well. Applying these notions (of 'finality' and 'universality') to the Sunna in addition to the Quran is more problematic than applying them to the Quran alone (which was the topic of the previous lecture). This is because Quranic verses containing regulations are generally minimalistic and ambiguous in their 'formulations', and they usually give the sense of the 'value' or 'essence' of the regulation; in contrast, regulations in the hadith literature are generally maximalist and highly contextual, and they rarely offer the 'values' or 'essences' of regulations.

Not only does the assumption of the 'finality' of 'the letter of the law' leave no room for refashioning of the 'forms' of regulations, but it also results in a very *exclusivist* and rigid understanding of the Sharia. This is because the accuracy and efficacy of the regulation is curtailed to its 'form' as defined in the hadith literature. This means that contracts, for instance, are not effective, and devotional acts cannot be deemed to have been discharged, so long as their exact 'forms' as specified in the hadith literature are not upheld and performed. Another effect of restricting the accuracy and efficacy of the regulation to the 'form' in the hadith literature is that the laws in non-Muslim lands pertaining to family law, such as marriage, divorce, financial settlements, and custody of children, are deemed to be ineffective. In fact, the assumption of the accuracy and efficacy being dependent upon the 'forms' of regulations as per the hadith literature *exclusively* has resulted in many scholars considering it a major sin to even engage with 'non-Islamic' law courts especially on issues pertaining to family law. Moreover, it seems that each Islamic sect considers referring to the Islamic courts of the other schools of fiqh as invalid.

It is surprising that despite asserting in our legal theory that regulations are based on rationally discernible 'values', we do not have the courage to re-evaluate the 'forms' of existing Sharia regulations no longer yielding their anticipated 'values'. The discourse on 'the principle of certainty' (and its legal authority and force) is the cause for this lack of courage, for it removes confidence from jurists. Thus, despite knowing that certain regulations do not make sense and are in fact regressive and counterproductive, we convince ourselves that they are sound by falling back upon 'the legal authority and force of certainty' and creating specious arguments and justifications which do not really make sense to us; subsequently, that which we know to be rational, ethical, and spiritual is deemed not to be so because it runs contrary to the 'form' of the original regulation.

Another substantial problem with the hadith literature is that it has regulations not mentioned in the Quran. As previously discussed, the Quran omits the regulation of stoning the adulterer to death and prescribes alternate 'forms' of punishment for adultery. However, a traditional Muslim mind will not be able to accept that Islam abrogated the pre-Quranic regulation of stoning adulterers to death, because the hadith literature contains spurious reports affirming the practice (of stoning adulterers to death). In the Islamic legal tradition, the hadith literature is regarded as being on par with the Quran as a source of regulations, in addition to being an exegesis of the Quran.

The real problem with the assumption of the 'finality' of the Sharia is not that it runs contrary to 'the existential property of growth' or that the Sharia's regulations will not cater for the growth of the human community adequately; rather, it undermines our confidence – that is, the confidence of today's twenty-first century Muslims – in the Sharia regulative system itself; for on the one hand, we intuit that numerous of its societal regulations are unfair and counterproductive, and on the other, we carry the belief that *the ḥalāl and ḥarām of Muhammad* is 'final' *until the Day of Qiyāma.*

Before discussing the topic of reformulating the Sharia regulations in accordance with their 'values' or 'essences', we will briefly discuss our view on how the relationship between the regulations of the Quran and those of the hadith ought to be. There are two basic hermeneutical (that is, interpretative) principles in our tradition that define the relationship between them. The first is 'the rejection of hadith reports conflicting with or contradicting the content of the Quran'. This principle is based on numerous Prophetic narrations in the hadith literature of both the major sects. The blessed Prophet realised that many falsities were being attributed to him, and so he gave the people a benchmark, a golden principle, by which they could distinguish between the true and false reports: 'Compare whatever is attributed to me with the Quran. If it complies with the Quran, accept it. If it runs contrary to the Quran, throw it against the wall.' This means that we must reject whatever contradicts, conflicts or is inconsistent with the Quran. The Imams affirmed this principle and stated that it also applied to their reports too.

The scope of this principle is not restricted to the regulations of the Sharia; it includes our theological understandings as well. We will mention a few examples of theological understandings that are rendered false when we compare them with the Quran. In both Sunni and Shia authentic hadith works (such as Sunan Ibn Mājah and al-Kāfī respectively), there are reports stating that the Quran is incomplete. Consider the following verses of the Quran: "Indeed We revealed the Reminder (the Quran), and indeed We are protecting it." (15:9) and "No falsehood can come to it (the Quran) from before it or behind it…". (41:42) Hence, there is a clear inconsistency and conflict between the Quran and hadith. Therefore, we are required to reject all such reports and uphold the verses of the Quran.

Similarly, texts assigning a 'demigod' status to the Imams must be rejected based on their inconsistency with the Quran. Consider the following caption from *al-ziyāra al-jāmiʿa* in which the reader is addressing the Imams: 'I bear witness that human beings' return will be to you, and they are accountable to you.' Now compare this with the following verse of the Quran: "… for only the delivery of the message is [incumbent] on you [O Muhammad], while calling [them] to account is Our [business]." (13:40) In light of this and numerous other verses of the Quran, the above text of *al-ziyāra al-jāmiʿa* and all other such texts have to be rejected. Obviously, if the blessed Prophet does not have the right to hold God's creatures to account, then by priority the Imams, who are inferior to the blessed Prophet in every sense, cannot be ascribed as having such a right, position, or status.

Another example of a hadith-based theological understanding conflicting with the Quran is the idea that all Muslim sects are bound for hellfire save one of them. In other words, there are reports stating that all Muslim faith groups are destined for damnation except one. A famous example is the report of 'the seventy-three sects', which assigns most Muslims to the Fire. Such reports have been used by each Muslim sect as a springboard to justify its own claim of *exclusivity* to the Truth and salvation, and to condemn all other sects. The result has been sectarianism for much of the history of Islam. Today, Muslim consciousness is infested with this sectarianism perhaps more than ever. When such reports are compared with the Quran, we understand their falsity and reject them outright. In the Quran, God offers salvation to all people regardless of their 'formal' religion (for instance, see 5:69).

As for Sharia regulations, this 'golden principle' gives us confidence to reject many unjust and draconian regulations that have crept into the Sharia. For instance, the regulation of stoning the adulterer to death; the Quran prescribes flogging as the punishment for adultery (see 24:2); it is only in the hadith literature that we find reports advocating the punishment of stoning to death. The Prophet has not stoned anyone to death to the best of our knowledge. The origin of the regulation of stoning gays to death and throwing them off cliffs is a report from Ibn Abbas in which he discusses the verses of the Quran citing the chastisement of the people of Sodom and Gomorrah.

Jurists have argued that hadith reports can be relied upon to derive regulations in areas where the Quran is silent. However, this claim is suspicious based on an incident in which a husband accused his wife of adultery without producing witnesses. The Prophet stated that the Quran did not have a regulation for such a case. He did not prescribe a novel punishment. Thereafter, a regulation was revealed stating that oaths must be taken from both the accuser and defendant in all such cases. Another example of an unjust and a draconian regulation which has crept into the Sharia is the regulation of apostasy. It is not mentioned in the Quran. Moreover, it is inconsistent with the Quranic principle of 'non-coercion' (see 2:256).

As stated, this 'golden principle' (which is 'to reject all reports that contradict, conflict or are inconsistent with the Quran') must also be applied to the hadith reports attributed to the Imams. In this respect, vast numbers of reports either cannot be substantiated beyond doubt as having been issued from them, or they are inconsistent with the Quran, or they mutually conflict and contradict each other. For instance, marrying women of the People of the Book is permitted by the Quran but prohibited by some reports and allowed by others.

The Quran often adopts a style that is general and ambiguous with regard to its formulations of societal regulations. For instance, the Quran is not clear at all regarding the right of the father to have custody over his children after a certain age, whereas the hadith literature presupposes it and supplies all the details. This style of generality and ambiguity adopted by the Quran is characteristic in almost all the societal issues it deals with. It becomes clear that its aim was to modify the status quo in Arab family and societal law, to express regulations in a way that was understandable to its initial audience, and yet to be general and ambiguous enough so that 'finality' could never be ascribed to them definitively. Philosophically, we know that it is impossible to ascribe 'finality' to regulations, just as it is impossible to ascribe 'finality' to any 'form' of manifested existence, because 'perpetual growth' is an 'essential' property of existence.

In conclusion thus far, we know that most hadith reports contradicting or conflicting with the regulations or ethos of the Quran can be rejected on the basis of the first hermeneutical principle, which is 'the rejection of hadith reports contradicting or conflicting with the content of the Quran'.

The second hermeneutical principle is 'the validity of all norms and regulations that are compliant with the Quran'. It is based on the following famous report of the blessed Prophet: "I leave two heavy-weights for you, one of which is greater than the other: The Book of Allah and my progeny, my Ahl al-Bayt." The blessed Prophet clarified that 'the Book' is the *heavier* of the two; hence, the progeny is the lighter of them. This means 'the Book' is *heavier* than 'the progeny' in terms of guidance and authority. Hence, scholars designate the guidance of 'the progeny' as being subordinate to the guidance of the Quran. We find that the Quran is minimalistic and more 'essence' based, whereas the hadith literature is maximalist, very detailed, and highly time-space bound (or contextual), and hence more 'form' based. In other words, hadith reports supplying societal regulations are contextual translations or 'formulations' of the general and ambiguous regulations in the Quran. This explains why authentic hadith are often found contradicting each other, such as in the case of the impurity of wine: The Quran is silent on the matter, implying that wine is pure in and of itself despite its consumption being prohibited; otherwise, it would not remain silent on the issue. Upon closer examination of the hadith literature, it becomes clear that the Imams were able to use the Quran's silence on the matter to issue the verdict of the impurity of wine for their vulnerable followers specifically, deterring them from all possible contact with wine. However, there are considerably more numbers of 'explicit' and 'strong' hadith reports designating wine as a pure substance, and there are significantly lesser numbers of 'non-explicit' hadith reports designating it as an impure substance.

The general and ambiguous style of the Quran is also exhibited in its 'formulations' of devotional regulations. In other words, its stipulations on the 'forms' of devotions are general, ambiguous, and lack detail. This creates the scope for a plurality of interpretations. For instance, the Quran does not provide the direction of washing the hands and arms during the minor ablution, hence any direction and sequence is permissible based on the aforementioned hermeneutical principles (the second one being 'the validity of all norms and regulations that are compliant with the Quran'). In view of this, the hadith reports of the Imams merely suggest 'the best practice'. They do not nullify the worth of the other 'forms' of ablution because the 'value' or 'essence' of the minor ablution is 'to induce a state of inner preparedness prior to worshipping God'. The Quran is also general, ambiguous, and lacks detail with regard to ṣalāt and hajj, creating the scope for a plurality of 'forms'. It should be noted that one of the aims of this current discussion is to make it clear that the 'essence' of regulations can be known by examining the 'forms' of regulations within the Quran and hadith literature. We will discuss this in more detail in due course.

We will now address those societal regulations in the Quran that most people today consider archaic because they are draconian and/or inconsistent with human dignity. Examples include the regulations mandating flogging and the severing of limbs, the regulation permitting the beating of disobedient wives, and the regulation stipulating half the share of inheritance for the woman. Undoubtedly, such regulations are a cause for concern so long as we insist they are 'optimal' and 'just' for people of all times and places, and therefore necessary for creating a virtuous society. Today, human reason considers the universal implementation of such regulations as unjust. It sees a direct conflict between these 'forms' in the Quran and the Quran's own emphasis that all human interactions be based on 'the principle of justice' and 'human nobility'. In other words, today's conscientious Muslims experience a conflict between 'reason' and 'revelation', or between 'the appreciation of the principle of justice in today's context' and 'the *forms* of societal regulations in the Quran'.

Sadr al-Din Muhammad Shirazi, known as Mulla Sadra (d. 1635-40), the mystic-philosopher, discussed the relationship between 'reason' and 'revelation' and expended considerable effort to prove the harmony existing between revelation, intuition, and reason. He argued that all three are modes of knowledge from God. There is a hierarchy between them in which revelation is the highest 'form' of knowledge and 'reason' the lowest. He argued that in light of the principles of 'the unity of existence' and 'the gradation of being' (which are two of the fundamental principles of his philosophy), all three — revelation, intuition, and reason — are simultaneously distinct from each other 'existentially' by virtue of their differing 'forms', and united with each other 'existentially' by virtue of their shared 'essence'; this is because they emanate from a single source and hence are 'made' of the same 'stuff' albeit in different 'forms'; thus, they must of necessity be in harmony with each other.

Developing on these conclusions of Mulla Ṣadra, we will explain the operations and significance of revelation, intuition, and reason in the domain of Sharia regulations. There are two points to bear in mind: Firstly, 'revelation as a text' is confined to a particular moment in time and space even though 'revelation as an actual experience' is the most superior 'form' or 'mode' of knowledge from God; in contrast, intuition and reason, as perpetually functioning faculties of the human soul, cannot be confined to a particular moment in time and space; as continually operating faculties, they are 'dynamic' in comparison to 'revelation as a text', which is 'static'; of course, the conclusions and judgements of the faculties of intuition and reason are also confined to particular moments in time and space and hence are also 'static'. Secondly, the faculties of intuition and reason are the only means to verify the truth and validity of 'revelation as a text'.

'Revelation as a text' consists of words communicated by God in a certain context; hence, its physical 'form' is fixed or crystallised. In contrast, intuition and reason are faculties that are perpetually operative in humans. As such, they are living realities subject to experience and growth with the passage of time. The following example serves to demonstrate this first point that 'revelation as a text' is fixed and restricted to its original 'form', whereas the faculties of intuition and reason are dynamic and subject to growth: At the time when the Quran prescribed half the share of inheritance for women, intuition immediately attested to its accuracy and fairness. This was followed by reason verifying and then justifying the intuitive knowledge by considering the regulation in the societal setup (of that time and place) in which men were the providers of women. Now when the same regulation is presented to Muslims today residing in Western settings, the faculty of intuition does not attest to its accuracy and fairness. This is followed by the faculty of reason verifying this intuitive judgement and then constructing the argument that the regulation does not give women their rightful share of inheritance in a social setup in which they are equal contributors to the household and are no longer provided for by men.

As for the second point that the faculties of intuition and reason are the only means to know and verify the truth and validity of 'revelation as a text', consider the following: When the Quran exhorted the Meccans to not lie, kill, and cheat, it made sense to them immediately at the intuitive level of their souls. Then after due consideration, reason verified that these instructions were productive, and that their contraries were unproductive. This is the reason why the Quran is named 'the Reminder', for it 'reminds' its listeners and readers of the Truth that is always available at the intuitive-existential level of the soul.

At the time of revelation, the faculties of intuition and reason were able to verify and justify every letter of the 'revelation as a text'. This is because the content of revelation was totally aligned with 'the existential property of growth', which meant that revelation as knowledge, and intuition and reason as tools for understanding and verifying that knowledge, were in sync with each other; hence, intuition and reason were able to verify and justify the content of 'revelation as a text'. This requires further explanation:

As stated previously, existence is dynamic. It is in a state of constant motion, from a state of weakness to strength. It is continually actualising its outer and inner potential and is always in a state of 'growth' outwardly (the manifested aspect of existence) and inwardly (the hidden aspect of existence). Hence, 'growth' is a property of existence, or an 'existential property'. This means all three modes of knowledge – revelation, intuition, and reason – are dependent upon and conditioned by the nature of existence: The content of 'revelation as a text' has to guide in accordance with 'the existential property of growth'; the faculty of intuition knows instantaneously that which is growth-promoting, wholesome, and holy, and its contrary; and human reason verifies that which is growth-promoting, wholesome, and holy, and its contrary, by constructing justifications and arguments. Therefore, whenever anything (including the contents of 'revelation as a text') is in line with 'the existential property of growth', the faculty of intuition will know and attest to its validity immediately without critical analysis. Then the faculty of reason will confirm the intuitive understanding based on evaluating data, after which it will construct proofs and arguments demonstrating that it is rationally, morally, and spiritually productive or growth-promoting.

Thus, intuition is an inner receptor that detects the 'growth' property of things, and reason is the mechanism of evaluating data and constructing justifications and arguments. In theory, the faculties of intuition and reason are always aligned. Therefore, whenever there is a misalignment between the three, the misalignment will be between a particular part of 'revelation as a text' and intuition/reason. Such misalignment simply indicates that the 'form' of a particular part of revelation is no longer in sync with 'the existential property of growth'. In other words, the misalignment shows that the 'form' (which was optimal for the context in which it was fashioned) is no longer optimal in facilitating the growth of the people of different contexts.

This is not something to be alarmed at. Verses of the Quran cited previously confirm that the reformulation of 'the *dīn* of Allah' has been an ongoing occurrence since the time of Prophet Nuh and more markedly from the time of Prophet Ibrahim. It will be recalled that the difference between devotional and societal regulations is that the 'forms' of devotional regulations are stipulated by the Divine and hence may fluctuate only slightly; whereas the 'forms' of societal regulations are modified as and when circumstances change and the collectivity grows. Thus, the societal regulations of revelation are totally beholden to the existential context and hence are fully discernible by reason, whereas the existential properties of the devotional regulations are only partially graspable by reason at present.

In summary, whenever intuition/reason and a particular part of the 'revelation as a text' become misaligned, we should know that we are not understanding that particular part accurately. That part of revelation was formulated for a particular context and was its remedy; however, the context changed subsequently, and so it is no longer the remedy for the new context; consequently, intuition/reason finds it difficult to verify that part, and so there is misalignment. It should be noted that that part of the revelation is 'eternal' and 'universally applicable' in and for its own context; however, beyond its own context, it is the 'essence' of that part of revelation that is 'eternal' and 'universally applicable', and not its 'form'. If we could somehow recreate the context in which revelation occurred, then that part of the revelation would still apply. In the future, if things regress to the degree that the initial context of the revelation is a reality once more and the existential aptitudes of the human soul match the initial audience of the revelation – for instance, if a war breaks out, God forbid, and we go back to living like seventh century Arabs – then in that case the societal regulations of the Quran would apply literally.

To reiterate, the societal regulations of the Quran apply eternally provided the context is the same. As soon as the context changes, there will be a misalignment between intuition/reason and 'revelation as a text', and so the 'forms' of the societal regulations of the Quran will no longer be optimal for the newer context. The faculty of reason will have to extrapolate the 'essences' of the societal regulations of the Quran and reformulate them into befitting regulations for the newer context. This will bring about alignment and equilibrium between 'revelation as a text' and intuition/reason.

Before reverting to the topic of regulations derived from the Quran and hadith, we need to explain the following issue:

How does the faculty of intuition grasp the 'rightfulness' or 'wrongfulness' of regulations, after which the faculty of reason is prompted to construct proofs and arguments to verify that intuitive knowledge? The main criterion in judging the 'rightfulness' or 'wrongfulness' of societal regulations is 'the principle of justice' as defined by the degree of growth of 'human nobility' of the collectivity in any given time and place. Justice is 'to put everything in its proper place' or 'to give everything its proper due', so that 'growth' remains optimal. Hence, 'justice' is the mechanism that ensures 'growth' in existence. Its 'forms' (individual, familial, communal, and societal) fluctuate according to the degree of growth of 'human nobility' of the individual and collectivity. This means a 'form' of 'the principle of justice' that is growth-promoting for a particular individual, family, community, or society may not be growth-promoting for another individual, family, community, or society due to the different degrees of growth of 'human nobility' between them; in other words, what is 'just' at one level of existence may not be 'just' at another level.

The expression 'human nobility' is used to denote that 'nobility' is the 'essence' of humankind. It refers to the sense of compassion, decency, and godliness within humankind, and as such it is in a constant state of refinement. What is acceptable at one stage of human life is not acceptable at another. For instance, the pocket money given to a ten-year-old child is increased incrementally as the age and demands of the child increase. To give a ten-year-old child an amount of pocket money that is sufficient for their needs is 'just', but to give the same amount to the same child at the age of fifteen who has far greater needs is 'unjust'. Similarly, it is acceptable for a five-year-old child to snatch food from across the table at dinner time because they lack a developed character and the moral sense that accompanies it, whereas the same behaviour is unacceptable from the same child at the age of fifteen.

Humankind as a whole is on the same trajectory of 'growth' in accordance with 'the existential property of growth' or 'evolutionary motion'. The dynamic nature of existence has resulted in the moral refinement of the human community (in addition to its rational and spiritual growth) through the course of its experiences. This means that the 'existential aptitudes' of humans (which refers to their psychological, cognitive, and moral aptitudes) have been changing, which is evinced by the different formulations of rights and regulations throughout human history. Therefore, we can confidently predict that today's system of human rights and duties will be outdated with passage of time, and so it will need updating.

Whenever something is out of sync or balance, including when the regulative system is misaligned with 'the principle of justice' and 'human nobility', the faculty of intuition within the soul immediately recognises it. In other words, whenever a regulation becomes unproductive or counterproductive, the faculty of intuition feels or senses it. Its function is *not* to understand fully, prove, or justify why certain regulations, traditions, or outlooks are wrong, rather its function is to feel, and hence know that they are wrong. This 'intuitive knowledge', or feeling of discontentment, prompts reason to investigate and examine the defects within a given regulation or cultural norm and subsequently construct explanations and proofs regarding its defectiveness, and arguments and justifications for its reformulation.

Usually enlightened individuals, such as prophets and sages expressed natural, societal, moral, and spiritual truths to their respective audiences, appealed to their faculties of intuition, and brought about societal reform. This is what happened in the case of the blessed Prophet. He said to his community: 'Do not kill, lie or cheat. Be kind to all and be true to your covenants'. He pointed out many unjust things in their system of rights, cultures, and outlooks. The people were able to affirm the truth of his message immediately because they already knew the 'wrongfulness' of their lifestyles *intuitively*. They felt and knew that things were not right but did not give that feeling and knowledge due attention and hence overlooked it.

In light of this, it is undeniable that Islamic regulations – be they devotional or societal – need updating in accordance with their underlying ethos or 'essences', the most basic of which is 'the existential property of growth'. At an intuitive level, we know certain regulations are not serving any purpose and others are counterproductive; however, prior to citing specific examples, consider how extraordinary the Islamic regulative system was in its own context.

All societal regulations of the Quran were radical and well ahead of their time as testified by their longevity. They were not merely aligned with 'the existential property of growth' and hence the best possible 'forms' for that time, rather they remained relevant for more than a millennium. Without prophetic intervention, the faculties of intuition and reason would only have been able to argue for and implement minimal societal changes as per 'the existential property of growth'. In contrast to this, the regulations of the Quran were so advanced that they enabled the Muslims to become the most advanced civilisation in the world within two centuries.

Consider the following very carefully: Women and orphans had no rights in the context of pre-Quranic Arabia. From its onset, the Quran emphasised their equal status, both in terms of their humanity and spirituality, which was shocking to the community. The Quran vehemently opposed the practice of burying daughters alive. It instituted a modest dress code for women whereby they were afforded a respectable identity and male minds were deterred from objectifying them. Moreover, the notion of 'modest covering' served to make women socially equal to males in that context. After that, they were given the rights of ownership and inheritance. The Quran and the blessed Prophet also addressed the pre-Quranic draconian and barbaric domestic treatment of women and modified it greatly; actually, it was no less than a paradigm shift: the pre-Quranic norm of severely chastising and killing women was replaced by the prophetic norm of counselling them and, if need be, reprimanding them by tapping their wrists. The aim of the Quran and Prophet was to modify the stagnant and unjust societal and familial regulations of pre-Quranic Arabia. They made them dynamic and 'just', and they put them on the right trajectory of evolution so that rights could be bestowed according to the growing 'aptitudes' of the individual and collectivity.

The punitive regulations of the Quran were considerably less draconian than the 'forms' of punishments meted out to offenders in pre-Quranic times. In their own context, these novel regulations were deemed to be fair, just, and in proportion to the crime committed. Remember the Quran could only legislate within the confines of its immediate context, and yet its regulations continued to contribute to the growth of the individual and collectivity for over a millennium. In the U.K., women could neither inherit nor divorce until as recently as a hundred years ago. Thieves were put to death in non-Islamic regions of the world for many centuries after Islam.

When we study the regulations of the Quran in their own context, we find that they were not only upgrading the pre-Quranic societal regulations and institutionalising standards in accordance with the 'existential aptitudes' of the people, but they were also transforming the community and driving it towards a greater sense of social justice, egalitarianism, and 'human nobility'.

It is unfortunate that Islamic regulations are understood in terms of their original 'forms' and not their 'essence', which is God-centricity and social justice. I have travelled across the world, and in almost every community, I have met women who have been abandoned by their husbands for years. These poor women have been unable to secure Sharia divorces from the highest Muslim legal authorities just because their husbands refuse to grant divorce, and in most of these cases it is obvious that the husbands' intentions are malicious. In many cases, the women have had civil divorces, and often, their husbands are blackmailing the women to pay tens of thousands of pounds in exchange for their permission to divorce. Despite knowing that such behaviour is morally reprehensible, Muslim legal authorities overlook such torture and extortion and do not grant divorces to the women due to their assumption of the 'finality' and 'eternality' of the 'form' of the regulation.

Are such decisions by our Muslim legal authorities 'just'? Do they accord with 'human nobility' today? No wonder people are becoming increasingly disenchanted with religion and its regulations. In contrast to this, the Quran advocates a Sharia of 'ease'. It states that its regulations are built upon this maxim of 'ease' and the maxim of 'no harm' and 'no hardship'; hence regulations are meant to be human friendly and non-coercive (see 2:185, 4:28, 5:6 and 22:78). These maxims are part of the Quran's foundations of societal regulations, alongside 'the principle of justice' and 'human nobility'. Muslim legal authorities have sacrificed these 'foundations' (or 'essences') of societal regulations to safeguard their 'forms' irrespective of whether the 'forms' are abusive, unjust, and/or counterproductive in the present context, and they do this on the basis of the assumption of the 'finality' of the literal 'form' and its optimal efficacy. The experience of abuse, injustice, and/or counterproductivity is prevalent in many societal regulations of the Sharia. Examples include the cutting of hands, flogging in public, not allowing mothers to have custody over their children after a certain age, and the partial inheritance for women.

In the domain of devotional regulations, the same attitude of the 'finality' and 'eternality' of the 'form' prevails, and hence there is an emphasis upon adhering to it as opposed to its 'essence'. This results in the belief of the *exclusivity* of a particular devotional 'form' and the rejection of all others. This belief is at the root of the attitude that has prevented Muslims from praying together in congregational worship to the One God. In contrast, the Quran and the blessed Prophet urged all the People of the Book (including the Muslims obviously) to unite in the worship of One God. The blessed Prophet was instructed to not be party to those who split into religious factions; however, Muslims today ignore his example by refusing to even pray together.

Imagine the crisis. How is this acceptable? Why should anyone be attracted to such a religion? The Prophet brought warring tribes and factions together and united them into a single community in the name of God. Imam al-Sadiq emphasised that the Muslim Umma should celebrate one day of Eid; however, Muslims celebrate it on different days because of their inability to see the 'essence' in and beyond the 'form'. Again, the 'essence' or 'spirit' of unity, community, and togetherness has been sacrificed for the sake of preserving the 'form'. Undoubtedly, if Muslims are still celebrating Eid on different days when Imam al-Mahdi arrives, he will advocate one day of Eid and bring unity among the different Muslim collectivities throughout the world. Consequently, the scholars will charge him with heresy.

Is it not ludicrous to designate sunrise and sunset as the markers for the beginning and end of the fast in regions of the world with abnormal days and nights? If someone fasts for four hours, would that classify as 'a fast'? Would it have any benefit for the body and mind? Would medical science classify it as 'a fast'? If someone fasts twenty-two hours every day for thirty consecutive days, would that classify as 'fasting with bearable difficulty'? Is it beneficial for the body and mind of an average person? The Quran states that 'bearable difficulty' is to be expected with regard to certain Sharia regulations. Will a nine-year-old child be able to bear fasting twenty hours every day for thirty consecutive days? Does fasting four hours every day for thirty consecutive days have any physical, psychological, or spiritual benefit?

Again, these problems stem from our acceptance of the assumption of 'finality' of the literal word of the regulation, be it in the Quran or hadith. There can be 'no-finality' to any 'form' in an evolutionary world, that is, in a world in which 'growth' is the property of existence. Accordingly, 'no-finality' is the cornerstone of the existential system – ontologically, epistemologically, psychologically, sociologically, technologically, and legally. However, 'finality' does belong to the 'essences' of societal regulations, such as 'the principle of justice' and 'human nobility', that are fashioned and refashioned continuously in differing contexts to create a well-balanced and moral community.

'Finality' also belongs to the specific and common 'essences' of devotional regulations and not their 'forms' strictly speaking; hence, their 'forms' can be tweaked too. We have several examples of devotional regulations being modified in both the Quran and hadith literature. For instance, the regulation of the obligation (*wujūb*) of performing the circumambulation (*ṭawāf*) between the Ka'ba and 'the standing place of Ibrahim' (*maqām Ibrāhīm*); Imam al-Baqir insisted that *ṭawāf* ought to be performed between the Ka'ba and *maqām Ibrāhīm*, for this was the practice during the life of the blessed Prophet. However, Imam al-Sadiq permitted the performance of *ṭawāf* beyond *maqām Ibrāhīm* due to the increased numbers of pilgrims during his imamate. In view of this, why is it difficult for us to accept the legitimacy of performing *ṭawāf* on the first, second, and third floors of *al-Masjid al-Ḥarām* during periods of the year when the numbers of pilgrims are in excess? Why must we continue to sacrifice a set number of animals in hajj even though it is impossible for pilgrims to consume even a percentage of the slaughtered animals during their days in Mina, resulting in the wastage of vast quantities of meat and the unjustified suffering of countless animals? The Quran prescribes the feeding of the poor and discontented in Mina alone. (22:36) Why can we not modify this devotional regulation and assist the needy beyond Mecca monetarily? Our 'human nobility' frowns upon such unnecessary and inhumane slaughter of animals. Similarly with fasting, Imam al-Sadiq permitted a girl who was experiencing excessive thirst to consume sips of water during her fast. This demonstrates that the 'essence' of fasting is 'meaningful abstention that is not excessively arduous', and hence he modified the 'form'. This means that the 'form' can be modified in accordance with 'existential aptitudes'.

Lecture Nine

The Plurality and Relativity of Collectivities

In these final lectures, we will elaborate on some verses of the Quran discussed previously. Recall the verse: "He it is Who sent His Messenger with guidance and 'the religion (*dīn*) of the Truth', that He might cause it to prevail over all religions (*dīn*), though the polytheists may be averse." (9:33) The previous verse ends with the phrase, "... though the *unbelievers* are averse". We want to analyse the meanings of the prophecy in the verse (that is, the prophecy of the prevalence of 'the *dīn* of the Truth' over all other *dīn*).

By utilising the terms 'unbelievers' and 'polytheists', it can be argued legitimately that both verses are confined to the immediate context of revelation. If this is the case, then the prophecy was fulfilled after the conquest of Mecca and hence during the lifetime of the blessed Prophet. However, the tone of the following portion of verse, "He has sent His Messenger with guidance and 'the *dīn* of the Truth' in order to cause it to prevail over all *dīn*..." (9:33), seems to be timeless even though the usage of the terms 'unbelievers' and 'polytheists' undeniably refers to specific groups of antagonists during the era of revelation. If this is the case, then "the prevalence of 'the *dīn* of the Truth' over all other *dīn*" is an eschatological prophecy. This interpretation is supported by eschatological material in the hadith literature, specifically those citing the second coming of the Messiah son of Mary, the appearance of Imam al-Mahdi, and the subsequent establishment of justice upon the earth. The content and language of these eschatological literatures take for granted that the final and optimal human community on earth will be diverse and plural religiously. The implication here is that both the 'essential' and 'formal' aspects of 'the *dīn* of Allah' will of necessity embrace the majority of humankind in all its diversity and plurality of 'forms'.

In previous lectures, we discussed the distinction between 'Islam' and '*islām*' in light of the Quran. Lowercase *islām* is a singular and fluid reality consisting of two components: the theoretical component, which is 'surrendering to God and His communication', and the practical component, which consists of devotional and societal regulations. Regarding the practical component, both types of regulations have been modified throughout human history so that they remain optimal in facilitating the growth of people of different contexts (that is, of people of different times and places). The issuance of devotional regulations is the prerogative of the Divine. Their purpose is to engender an attitude of God-centricity and to bestow and strengthen a sense of religious identity in individuals adhering to them. Societal regulations address human interactions. As such, they are based on reason, 'the principle of justice', 'human nobility', and the maxims of 'ease', 'no harm' and 'no hardship', and are subject to the existential condition of humankind as humankind in any given time and place. Islam – by which is meant the 'formal' organised religion that we follow – is an expression of *islām*, for it originated in a particular time and place.

If the phrase "the *dīn* of the Truth" in the verse (being discussed) refers to Islam as it seems to do – that is, if Islam is to prevail over all other *dīn* – then Islam must of necessity be as flexible and fluid as *islām* for it to be able to embrace the plurality and diversity of the other 'forms' of *islām*, as per the eschatological literature. In other words, its theology and ever-evolving societal regulations will have to acknowledge all God-centric faiths and spiritualities as legitimate expressions of its 'essence' and hence alternative means to God.

It should be noted that the notion of the prevalence of Islam (over all other *dīn*) also has the connotation of it being the last 'form' of *islām* to be revealed, and of it being based upon the final revelation. This 'finality' means that neither Islam nor its revelation will be superseded by another divinely revealed religion or revelation respectively.

Unlike previous prophets, the blessed Prophet Muhammad was able to convey both *islām* and its 'form', Islam, by means of the Quran and his narrations. Islam primarily addressed the bodily and psychological needs of the people of the time. In contrast, *islām* is 'the one *dīn* of Allah' that has expressed itself repeatedly in different 'forms' since the time of Prophet Adam, and it will continue to subsist until the end of humankind's journey on earth. The blessed Prophet was successful in integrating the fluidity and dynamism of 'the *dīn* of Allah' within Islam. Consequently, he has ensured that Islam, as the final expression of *islām*, can accommodate both human plurality and evolution until the Day of Judgement.

We will now examine the 'formal' aspect of both *islām* and Islam. The Quran states that diversity is an existential norm for it was ordained to be part and parcel of the Design in the creation of humankind:

> *We have revealed to you [O Muhammad of] the Book with the truth, as a confirmation of what came before It of the Book (Torah and Gospel), and as a sure witness over it… We have assigned a law and a path to each of you. If Allah willed, He would have made you one people, but He wanted to test you in what He has given you. So compete [with each other] in good deeds… (5:48)*

God has willed 'diversity' so that He may witness the performance of good works. Hence, 'diversity' is an existential prerequisite for the performance of good works according to this verse. Now consider the following verse: "Had your Lord willed, He could have made humankind into one people [*umma*], and yet they would not cease differing [with each other about things]." (11:118) Thus, difference amongst people, and their tendency to differ amongst themselves in respect of their appreciation and leanings, would exist even if they all belonged to same nation (*umma*) and regarded each other as ancestrally related. The verse which follows this verse implies that this tendency to be different and differ is innate and cannot be removed "save for one upon whom your Lord is merciful..." (11:119) These two verses are stating the negative side of 'difference' in the context of a single nation. However, the verse cited prior to these (that is, 5:48) and several others (some of which have been cited in previous lectures) discuss 'diversity' positively as part of the design of creation, for instance: "O humankind, We have created you from a male and a female, and made you nations and tribes that you may know each other. Verily, the noblest among you with Allah is the most God-conscious of you. Indeed, Allah is All-knowing, All-aware." (49:13) and "Among His signs is the creations of the heaven and the earth and the difference of your languages and your colours. Surely in that are signs for those who know." (30:22)

Therefore, 'diversity' is an existential property created by God, which means that the demand for absolute uniformity at any level of existence and in any aspect of human life is not only unrealistic, but it is contrary to the intent of God and hence an impossible task existentially. History has demonstrated that the imposition of strict uniformity upon people has always resulted in extremely negative and often devastating outcomes. Hence, the Quran and the blessed Prophet embraced 'diversity' and sought 'unity' in 'diversity' based on commonalities therein. Before citing examples of how the blessed Prophet embraced religious diversity and considered it to be a natural and obvious part of 'the *dīn* of Allah', and how the early Muslim conquerors accepted, respected, and gave rights to non-Abrahamic communities residing within the Islamic rule, we will briefly explain the existential basis for 'plurality'.

In his philosophy of the nature of existence, Mulla Sadra advocates the principle of 'the individuation of existent entities'. This principle is deceptively simple. Everything is one existent, that is, everything is an individual. Each human being is one human, and each tree is just one tree. Multiplicity and numbers exist in the mind alone. 'Two', 'three', and 'four' are mental concepts or 'forms' of the mind. When we state the phrase 'two apples' for instance, the notion of 'two-ness' or 'the quality of being two' exists in the mind alone, because outside the mind there is 'one apple' and 'another individual apple', that is, there is just 'one-ness' or 'the quality of being one' outside the mind. Everything in the 'seen' realm of existence has its own specific 'form' to which it is confined. Therefore, each thing can only be itself and an individual.

Similarly, universal notions are also mental concepts. A universal notion, such as the term 'human being', which embraces all eight billion of us, emerges in the mind as a result of its observation of the core properties that a group of individuals have in common. The core properties shared by the individuals of a universal notion are termed as the 'essence' of the universal. Despite the notion of 'human being' being a 'universal' with an 'essence' shared by all its individuals, it also serves to distinguish itself from other universal notions within the animal kingdom, even though all such universal notions share the 'essence' of 'being an animal' or animality. The point to note here is that universal notions and their 'essences' do not nullify the individuality and uniqueness of their respective individuals. In other words, a universal notion, such as 'human being', does not negate the existential 'difference' and 'diversity' between all its individuals that makes each one of them a unique individual. This means that despite being equally 'human' by virtue of sharing the same 'essence', individuals are of different persuasions and differ in their likes and dislikes. Hence, we react to situations differently and have different 'aptitudes'.

Consider the following: Nationality simultaneously unites the people of one nation and differentiates them from the people of other nationalities, and yet within any given nationality, people differ in terms of religion and profession. The same is true for the notions of 'ethnicity', 'culture' and 'religion', which are broader and transcend the notion of 'nationality', and where each has several different universals within it. For instance, notions such as 'Khoja', 'Pakistani', 'West Indian', and 'British' are examples of universals within the notion of 'culture'. Each universal simultaneously unites its individuals and differentiates them from the individuals of other universals; and all individuals within a given universal are diverse, distinct, and unique.

Therefore, each of us is an individual existentially, that is, in terms of our bodies and psychology (or our inner world of thought, feeling, and will). We form groups to which we identify and belong, based on commonalities in our bodily aspects (or shared bodily properties), such as ethnicities, cultures, and nationalities. We also form groups (to which we identify and belong) based on commonalities in our outlooks, philosophy, ethics, morality, and behaviour, such as religions and political parties. Yet as individuals, we also live in very private subjective worlds: our sense perception, thinking, interacting, and feeling have the element of being individual and subjective. Thus, no two individuals are the same, and yet they are the same. No two people share the same God, and yet they share the same God.

In our bodily-worldly existence, we do not exist outside the boundaries of collective bodies. In other words, human beings can never be free of 'the collectivity' in this world, be it the family, community, society, nation, or humankind. We take birth inside a family unit. Families unite and form a community based on shared interests. Communities come and work together and form a society. Different societies coalesce and form a nation, and then nations unite and form the global human community based on shared interests. After the establishment of institutions addressing the global concerns of humankind, 'human reason' in light of 'human nobility' recognises the necessity for universal human standards based on our shared humanity. From an existential perspective, we humans have formed greater groupings and umbrella organisations as a result of our existential condition of evolutionary growth. In other words, the greater groupings and umbrella organisations are a necessary outcome of human growth and evolution, and they are necessary for the actualisation of human potential.

Therefore, individuality is the basis of our unique personalities, differentiating us from each other, and yet we are all very similar. Hence, we belong to several collectivities simultaneously, ranging from the family unit to the global human community. Human reason in light of 'human nobility' has conceived of greater and broader notions unifying humankind based on common shared interests; the most fundamental of these common shared interests is the universal existential desire within humankind to continually actualise its potential. At the same time, human reason in light of 'human nobility' understands that the actualisation of humankind's potential depends upon safeguarding and honouring the individuality and uniqueness of the human individual.

Therefore, human beings are individuals in their personal and private capacities, and they are collectivities with respect to their bodily-worldly needs and other rational considerations. They form lesser and greater groupings based on their shared interests, outlooks, and humanity. Hence, every individual coexists simultaneously with the lesser and greater collectivities to which they belong.

Obviously, the blessed Prophet was mindful of the existential reality of 'the individual as an individual' and 'the individual as part of lesser and greater collectivities'. Hence, the Quran stipulates the maxim of 'no coercion in religion' to safeguard and honour our existence at the level of the individual; in other words, the maxim of 'no coercion in religion' respects and preserves the individuality and uniqueness of the human individual. The Prophet said that Salman and Abu Dharr worship the same God differently, despite both adhering to the same faith and teachings. This narration presupposes the maxim of 'no coercion in religion' and that individuality is at the root of humankind's relationship with God. This individual and unique relationship between every human being and God is the reason why the Quran does not limit its soteriology to the adherents of any one particular 'formal' faith or religion. In other words, 'salvation' is only contingent upon an individual's private relationship with God according to the Quran.

The Quran uses the word 'Muslims' towards the end of the revelatory era to refer to the collectivity of individuals adhering to the Sharia of Prophet Muhammad. It exhorts the collectivity of 'the People of the Book', including the Muslims, to recognise that they are one collectivity by virtue of their respective devotions to One God; in other words, all the Abrahamic faiths are united because they all worship One God, even though each faith is different to the others and diverse within itself. Finally, the blessed Prophet affirmed the collectivity beyond the collectivity of monotheistic religions in his famous Medinan charter or constitution. This greater collectivity included pagans as well as the People of the Book on account of their shared humanity. It united all the people of Medina on the basis of their common interests and made them into one people. Yet each collectivity within this greater collectivity was given the right to self-determination; hence, each one adjudicated its own internal affairs in accordance with its own tribal or religious regulations. This is akin to the phenomenon of sects within Islam; each has its own unique interpretation, jurisprudence, art, and cultural events, and yet the identity of the '*umma*' and the ritual of hajj serve to bind them all together.

Therefore, the Prophet was very much aware of the dynamics between the individual and the various degrees of the collectivity. His dedication to *tawḥīd* (One-ness) made him very proactive in accommodating all the different collectivities, as evinced in the Quran and hadith literature. His blessed example in this regard demonstrated that Islam is meant to be as fluid as *islām*.

We have discussed at length how the blessed Prophet welcomed and accommodated the People of the Book, but how about individuals who are sincere, practicing believers but do not belong to the Abrahamic faiths? Can Islam accommodate individuals who belong to religions and faiths other than the Abrahamic ones? How about individuals who are sincere, practicing monotheists but do not belong to any organised faith or religion?

Early Muslim migrants settled in India and China. After acquainting themselves with the religious systems of these great regions thoroughly and deeply, they concluded that Hindu philosophy, Buddhism, Taoism, and Confucianism were 'essentially' monotheistic. Thus, these Muslim migrants classified the adherents of these religions and religious philosophies as 'the People of the Book'. As for the non-monotheistic religions in these regions, their attitude was one of inclusion and harmonious coexistence as per the precedent set by the Medinan Charter of the blessed Prophet which included everybody, including the pagans.

It should be noted that the problem with the polytheists of Mecca who were opposing the blessed Prophet was that they were self-confessed 'enemies of Allah' and 'enemies of the *dīn* of Allah'. Being an 'enemy of the *dīn* of Allah' would be akin to being an enemy of the state today. This is because 'the *dīn* of Allah' consists of societal regulations in addition to devotional regulations and the 'essence', which is God-centricity; hence, a person opposing the societal regulations would classify as an 'enemy of the *dīn* of Allah' even if they performed the devotional regulations and subscribed to a God-centric worldview, like some of the Jewish and Christian tribes in Medina during the Medinan period of the life of the Prophet. This is the reason why the verse of Sūra al-Tawba (see 9:29) instructs the faithful to combat those People of the Book who were not upholding 'the *dīn* of the Truth'.

In view of this and the maxim of 'non-coercion', agnostics and atheists cannot be termed as 'the enemies of God' as long as they are genuinely unconvinced about the existence of God, or they are genuinely convinced about the non-existence of God, respectively. They must be included within the broader collectivity, the basis of which is shared humanity, as per the precedent set by the Medinan Charter, so long as they abide by the societal regulations of 'the *dīn* of God'. As noted in previous lectures, the Quran narrates that Prophet Yusuf took his brother Binyamin into his custody in accordance with 'the *dīn* of the king' (see 12:76). Here, 'the *dīn* of the king' signifies the 'formal' socio-political-economic system of Egypt. Obviously, Prophet Yusuf did not worship idols, and so his participation in 'the *dīn* of the king' signifies abiding by the societal regulations of Egypt under the political authority of the king. Similarly, Islam must readily acknowledge agnostics and atheists as part of the broader collectivity so long as they are willing to abide by its societal regulations.

What is needed is a Sharia outlook and framework that yields a dynamic societal system which can facilitate the growth of a 'pluralistic' human community. It is inconceivable that the Mahdi will institute the *jizya* (the tax for non-Muslims) for the Abrahamic community given that notions of equal citizenship and inalienable human rights are increasingly becoming the norm in nation states with Muslim majority populations in the twenty-first century. Thus, it is necessary for a Sharia theory that distinguishes between devotional and societal regulations as discussed previously. Devotional regulations are contingent upon religious texts. In contrast, societal regulations are not contingent upon religious texts per se, and hence are 'non-religious' or 'secular' essentially. They can be formulated by human reason alone – that is, independently of religious texts – in accordance with its own experiences, 'the principle of justice', 'human nobility', and other legal maxims. In other words, human reason can conceive and generate the best possible societal regulations after due consideration irrespective of whether one has faith or not.

Therefore, societal regulations supplied by God must be understood holistically as a divine intervention laying the groundwork for the post-revelatory state of humankind in which experience, reason, 'the principle of justice', 'human nobility', and other legal maxims organise the lives of humans on the basis of 'the existential property of growth'. Political systems of governance, societal setups, and economic and commercial models have always been and continue to be conceived of in and for different contexts by humans with differing 'existential aptitudes' via reason, 'the principle of justice', and so on. Historically, religions merely tweaked pre-existing systems of governance, societal setups, and economical and commercial models in accordance with 'the principle of justice', 'human nobility', and other legal maxims. These modifications were then affirmed by the faculties of intuition and reason of their respective audiences.

At this point, several questions are likely to have arisen in the mind of the reader, including:

1. How can a Sharia theory that renders societal regulations as essentially 'non-religious' or 'secular' be correct? In other words, how can a theory that admits to the existence of regulations devoid of any essential 'Islamic' character be valid?

2. Can we ever be sure that rationally deduced societal regulations are as accurate and acceptable to God as the societal regulations in the Quran?

3. How can a theory that admits to the relativity of regulations be correct? In other words, can a theory that allows for different regulations in differing contexts be correct?

4. How can a theory that does not admit to any stable regulations be correct? In other words, can a theory that does not accept the 'finality' of any regulations be correct?

The first question is concerned with the 'secular' nature of societal regulations and their being devoid of any essential 'Islamic' character. The word 'secular' for our consumption does not mean, imply, or have anything to do with the denial of the existence of God. It is an adjective describing the fact that the methods employed by jurists in the formulation of societal regulations utilise human reason, 'the principle of justice', 'human nobility', and other legal maxims as opposed to religious texts. It is also used to describe the fact that societal regulations are derived by human reason, 'the principle of justice', 'human nobility', and other legal maxims. This is exactly what the blessed Prophet was commanded to do as evinced by the Quran: to establish a society based on 'the principle of justice' and 'human nobility' in that time and place. The fact that the societal reforms of the Prophet appealed to his initial audience is itself an evidence that they were based upon human reason, 'the principle of justice', and 'human nobility'. Furthermore, the Prophet issued regulations only to the extent required by his own context, which is why there has never been a set or defined 'form' of governance, political system, model of commerce and economics, or legal system throughout Muslim history. At the time of the blessed Prophet, he and/or the divine agencies (of the revelation) merely applied 'the principle of justice' to the immediate context and suggested befitting models for that time.

Therefore, the societal regulations of the Sharia are 'secular' in principle. For instance, the regulation of *zakāt* or income tax, which caters for the needs of the poor among other things, is an essential part of any welfare system and is based upon human reason, 'the principle of justice', and 'human nobility', and as such it is found within both theocracies and non-theocracies. In fact, on the issue of *zakāt*, the Prophetic outlook suggests that a correlation exists between the morality and spirituality of a society and the degree to which that society ensures that the basic needs of its individuals are catered for. The distinctly 'Islamic' character of the *zakāt* pertains to its voluntary 'spiritual' component, which is to perform the act with the attitude of care for the 'other' and the intention of seeking proximity to Allah. This inner or subjective component relates to the individual's salvation, since the *zakāt* will fulfil its 'outer' function of contributing to the welfare of the collectivity irrespective of whether the individual performs the act with the attitude of care and the intention of seeking God's proximity or not. It should be noted that the cultivation of the virtue of care and the spiritual attitude of seeking God's proximity is the main objective of the teachings of Islam, and hence it is an intrinsic part of its educational system. Thus, the attitude of caring for the 'other' together with the intention of seeking God's proximity is supposed to accompany every human act. However, the virtue of care, the spiritual attitude of seeking God's proximity, and the degree of their cultivation, are not criteria for evaluating societal regulations or the rights of individuals.

The second question is concerned with whether it is possible to have 'surety' that the 'secular' or rationally deduced societal regulations are accurate and acceptable by God. The topic of 'certainty' is central in the Shia legal tradition. It stems from the idea that we, as Muslims, are required to obey the regulations of God, and so we must be 'certain' or 'sure' that the regulations we are following are 'the intended regulations of God'; otherwise, it would be possible for God to have a reason to punish us on the Final Day.

This legal outlook is based on the belief of a fixed ontology, that is, it presupposes that existence does not undergo any change and is fixed eternally. As such, there is no dynamism or evolution in the human condition. From this it follows that regulations must also be universal, eternal, and immutable, and that the 'forms' of regulations in the Quran and hadith literature must be optimal forever, such as the regulation of the cutting of the hand of the thief. Accordingly, the face-value appreciation of the Quran and hadith literature is sufficient in supplying 'the regulations as intended by God'. However, the assumption of an eternally fixed state of existence is inaccurate. The dynamic nature of existence and humankind is made clear by the fact that the *sharias* of former prophets were abrogated fully or in part by subsequent ones, and later regulations of the Quran abrogated former ones.

Therefore, the dynamic nature of existence and humankind means that regulations cannot be said to be fixed eternally. God has issued different regulations for people of different times and places, and He has abrogated regulations during the lifetime of the blessed Prophet, which shows that regulations are a 'means' to an end and not 'ends' in themselves. The purpose of God's issuance of instructions and guidance in the form of regulations is to facilitate our growth to Him. Thus, God changed or abrogated His Own regulations when they were not facilitating growth, or in other words, when they were no longer 'optimal' in facilitating the growth of the individual and collectivity.

Therefore, the fundamental criterion in determining whether a 'form' of a regulation is acceptable to God and hence intended by Him is if that 'form' is optimal in facilitating the rational, moral, and spiritual growth of the individual and collectivity. This is the benchmark by which human reason can assess the efficacy of regulations, and then modify or reformulate them if need be. As soon as a 'form' of a regulation is no longer optimal in facilitating the growth of the individual and collectivity, and human reason can conceive of another newer 'form' that is definitively 'optimal', then it is necessary to replace it with the newer 'form'. However, as soon as the newer, optimal 'form' of a regulation is being adhered to, it must be kept in mind that it too may become outdated due to the dynamic nature of existence. In other words, the 'forms' of all regulations must be deemed to be 'fallible' in this realm of existence which is inherently dynamic and evolutionary. The 'form' of every regulation is to be considered 'infallible' in and for its immediate context only.

It has been a common occurrence throughout the history of Islamic law that a 'form' of a regulation conceived by one jurist has alternative 'forms' conceived by other jurists. Such is the nature of human understanding and knowledge: The progression of knowledge is dependent upon a scholar's individual experiences and endeavours together with healthy disagreements with other scholars. Therefore, the formulation of the most accurate and optimal regulation is also dependent upon a jurist's individual experiences and endeavours together with healthy disagreements with other jurists.

In the areas of systems of governance, commerce, and economics, we Muslims are constantly trying to ascertain the validity or invalidity of emerging models by seeking their precedent in the 'forms' of regulations fashioned by the blessed Prophet. However, the 'forms' of regulations fashioned by him are the result of applying 'the principle of justice', whose appreciation is subject to the degree of growth of 'human nobility' of that time and place, to the prevailing modes of governance, commerce, and economics in seventh century Arabia. Hence, it is unlikely that any precedent exists in prophetic times that can truly validate or invalidate contemporary systems of governance, commerce, and economics; and more importantly it is not even necessary that there be any precedent to validate or invalidate today's norms, for he merely applied 'the principle of justice and 'human nobility' to the pre-existing norms to ascertain whether they were optimal, and to modify them if they were not.

It has always been the function of human reason to conceive of and then formulate societal regulations. In like manner, both revelation and the Prophet formulated optimal 'forms' of societal regulations for the people of their immediate context on rational bases; otherwise, their primary audience would not have assented to what they were hearing and would have rejected their guidance altogether. In fact, the faculty of human reason is our only means to knowledge and growth, and Muslims have demonstrated its utility and mastery in every conceivable domain from the onset of the post-prophetic era until the sixteenth century.

If Imam al-Mahdi issues 'optimal' regulations for his followers when he reappears, then even he will be beholden to human reason and principles, such as 'the existential property of growth', 'the principle of justice', and 'human nobility'; for otherwise, the people will not be able to assent to their accuracy and hence will reject them. Moreover, even Imam al-Mahdi's regulations will be 'fallible' and need modifications or upgrading at some point after they are issued due to existential dynamism.

The third question is concerned with the 'relativity' of regulations. The rate and degree of growth of a group and its existent entities is 'relative' when compared to the rate and degree of growth of other groups and their respective existent entities. In other words, the degree of growth of a collectivity and its individuals will be different to the degree of growth of other collectivities and their respective individuals. Therefore, the 'relativity' of regulations is a natural consequence of the differing rates and degrees of growth of different collectivities; for instance, some collectivities will have 'grown' more rationally than others, and some collectivities will have 'grown' more morally than others.

The existence of 'relativity' between collectivities is presupposed, and hence affirmed, by both revelation and the Prophet: for instance, both exhorted the People of the Book to implement the societal regulations of their respective faiths; and yet each individual residing in Medina was also required to abide by the more general societal regulations of the collectivity that embraced all the citizens of Medina irrespective of faith. This demonstrates the existence of 'relativity' between different religious collectivities and the fact that they can unite upon commonalities between them and form a greater collectivity, which will have regulations applying to all the individuals of the smaller collectivities within its ambit.

The final question pertains to 'the principle of no-finality', specifically the issue of 'no-finality' with respect to the 'forms' of devotional and societal regulations. In an evolutionary universe like ours, nothing can be 'final' or 'absolute' because all entities are in a constant state of flux. In other words, the 'forms' of all things are subject to perpetual change, which means that 'finality' can never be ascribed to any particular 'form'. Only the Absolute – that is, only Allah – is 'absolute' and 'final', and hence eternal and immutable. Therefore, 'no-finality' is an *essential* property of everything other than Him. Simply put, 'no-finality' is the absolute norm of existence, and hence it embraces all material entities. The cosmos is in a constant process of self-revelation; it is always revealing itself in different, greater, and more elaborate ways. To reiterate, 'no-finality' is the result of the incessant evolutionary motion of existent entities, which means that 'finality' can never be ascribed to the 'form' of anything whatsoever.

Mulla Sadra terms this perpetual 'growth' as 'substantial motion' to convey the fact that the nature of existence is 'motion'. However, he does not mean 'motion' in the ordinary sense of movement in time and space; rather, he means the transmutation of the substance in the sense of the evolution of the soul of a fertilised ovum and its *visible* 'form', which is the observable fertilised ovum, into the soul of a child and its *visible* 'form', which is the perceivable body of the child, or the transmutation of the soul of a seed and its *visible* 'form', which is the tangible seed, into the soul of a tree and its *visible* 'form', which is the solid tree. Thus, motion is not restricted to the bodily, material, visible, 'formal', or 'outer' only; rather, it occurs simultaneously in both the 'outer' and 'inner' aspects of all things, including humans. This is the reason why the on-going refinement in 'human nobility' and its appreciation of 'the principle of justice' and morality is observable from one era to next.

Changes in the psychological makeup of humankind, which is the content of the soul, (such as the changes in 'human nobility' and its appreciation of 'the principle of justice' and morality) are among the main reasons why change has occurred in societal setups, modes of governance, and systems of rights. Compare the psychological makeup of past peoples who considered the rule of 'might is right' to be normal with the psychological makeup of humans today who consider 'inalienable human rights' to be natural; or compare the content of the soul that justified wars and indecencies in the name of pagan religions with the content of the soul that rejects such religions and their deities on the basis of the innate sense of compassion, decency, and godliness in humankind (or 'human nobility').

Therefore, we conclude that 'substantial motion', which produces change in both the outer and inner aspects of existence and humankind, was the cause for the various *sharias* of the prophets being tailored according to the degree of the 'existential aptitudes' prevalent in their respective audiences; hence, each *sharia* was different to the others, and yet each was optimal in facilitating the growth of the people it was addressing. When a community had 'grown' significantly in terms of its 'existential aptitudes' such that it required a new *sharia*, then a new optimal *sharia* would be revealed. This is evinced by the phenomenon of successive revealed *sharias*. Thus, today's Sharia has to mirror the 'existential aptitudes' of humankind today. The psychological makeup/content of the soul of today's humans is vastly different to the makeup/content of the soul of the seventh century pagan Arab in terms of 'existential aptitudes'.

It cannot be argued thus: 'it is false to state that the Sharia was tailored to the 'existential aptitudes' and the degree of 'human nobility' of the pagan Arabs, since they lacked both (existential aptitudes and 'human nobility') at the time of revelation'. This is because those pagan Arabs were able to: firstly, intuit the truth of the content of the Sharia of the Prophet Muhammad; secondly, justify it with human reason; thirdly, embrace it as opposed to the *sharias* of the other Abrahamic faiths which they were already familiar with; and finally, 'grow' through it. This affirms the fact that they were ready internally to receive a *sharia* that would facilitate their 'growth' into a nobler state of existence.

Prior to concluding this lecture, we will briefly elaborate on the idea of the on-going refinement of 'human nobility'. The Quran states that God breathed His Spirit into Adam (see 15:29). Since everything in existence seeks to complete and perfect itself perpetually, the Spirit in humankind also yearns constantly to return to its Origin (which is its completion and perfection). The Quran refers to the incessant motion of return to the Origin in the following verse: "Indeed, We belong to Allah, and to Him we [are in a constant state of] return." (2:156) 'Returning to God' cannot be 'bodily' obviously. It pertains to the soul and the Spirit, and hence the soul must grow and become good and godly, as discussed in previous lectures (for instance, see 84:6). The expression 'human nobility' refers to both the state of 'being godly' or godliness and the unending process of 'becoming godly'. Kindness, generosity, fairness, and altruism are aspects of godliness and thus are facets of 'human nobility'. Throughout history, there have always been individuals who have attained the state of godliness or 'being godly' and hence have reached the summit of 'human nobility', such as the blessed prophets, imams, and sages. In contrast, the state of 'human nobility' of any given 'collectivity' is in an unending process of 'becoming godly'.

Consider the following verse: "Indeed, We have ennobled the Children of Adam." (17:70) Humankind is noble and sanctified by virtue of the Spirit of God within. Hence, it has this sense of nobility and sanctity. The emergence of this innate 'human nobility' is subject to the evolutionary motion of the soul on account of the Spirit being enmeshed with 'the bodily'. This means the emergence of godliness is dependent upon bodily experience in this realm.

Since the 'existential aptitudes' and the sense of nobility and sanctity in both the individual and collectivity are evolving and being continually refined, there can be no 'finality' to any 'form' of socio-economic or political system, nor to any 'form' of regulation irrespective of whether it is legal, rational, moral, societal, religious, or secular. Inevitably, all 'forms' will have to be tweaked or replaced by newer ones in accordance with 'existential aptitudes' and 'the principle of justice' as defined by the degree of 'growth' of 'human nobility'.

It should be noted that 'human nobility' and 'the principle of justice' are related to the faculties of intuition and reason respectively:

•   'Human nobility' refers to the innate sense of compassion, decency, and godliness of the soul. It is the 'essence' of the human soul and hence the ground of the faculty of intuition (of knowing right and wrong, truth and falsehood, and so on) and all the other faculties. In other words, the operation of the faculty of intuition depends upon the actualisation of 'human nobility'. Moreover, the efficacy of the faculty of intuition varies in accordance with the degree of 'growth' or actualisation of 'human nobility'.

•   'The principle of justice' is a rational mechanism utilised by human reason in light of the knowledge of the faculty of intuition to evaluate, modify, and justify existing rights and regulations, and to derive and justify new rights and regulations in accordance with differing 'existential aptitudes'.

Thus, the real determiner of what is right and wrong is the faculty of intuition, whose accuracy (of what is right and wrong) depends upon the degree of the actualisation of the 'human nobility' of the soul; whereas 'the principle of justice' is utilised by human reason, in light of the knowledge of the faculty of intuition, during the process of deriving, evaluating, modifying, or justifying rights and regulations. This will be discussed in more detail in future series of lectures, God willing.

Finally, we will mention a few points on the agency responsible for formulating the Sharia in the absence of the Mahdi and in light of our earlier discussions on the 'finality' of the revelation. God's aim in bestowing the 'vicegerency' (*khilāfa*) of the earth to the children of Adam is to enable us to 'grow' to the fullness of our potential so that we become needless of teachers and instructors. God has vested us with His nature. His nature is manifesting Itself through the ways in which we think and behave. Consider the following analogies: The aim of our formal education system is to make the student sufficiently competent so that they become needless of their instructors. Children come of age with experience, guidance, and learning so that the parent no longer needs to hold their hands.

The phenomenon of successive revelations and *sharias* is no different. Textbooks — as brilliant as they may be — are there to serve the educational needs of students. Hence, they are subordinate to the linguistic, cultural, rational, ethical, and psychological makeup of the students. The aim of revelation and the Sharia has always been to aid the human community to reach the prophetic stage of self-actualisation. In other words, humankind is supposed to 'grow' to a stage where it becomes needless of external interventions. This is what is anticipated by our creation, and it constitutes the success of humankind. If we achieve this, then God will exhibit utmost pride. Did He not say to the angels, "Surely, I know what you do not know!" (2:30), after they expressed our unsuitability as His 'vicegerents', citing our bad traits to Him? Imagine, despite all our killing, pillaging, and corruption, we humans will come of age and display such gems of godliness and splendour as is unimaginable.

Therefore, the agency responsible for the formulation of Sharia regulations will be the collective human mind. As discussed previously, societal regulations must be scrutinised constantly in light of 'the principle of justice' and 'human nobility', and they are to be reformulated in accordance with them as and when necessary. Insofar as this is done, they will qualify as 'forms' of the 'essence' of the societal regulations of the Quran. Devotional regulations can also be reformulated if drastic changes in the context render the performance of devotional acts untenable or extremely difficult; however, their reformulation is permitted only to the extent required to safeguard their 'values' or 'essences'. Imagine if humankind migrates to a distant planet in the future that has a different day and night cycle, longer or shorter years, multiple moons, and no Qibla, then the devotional regulations will need to be reformulated in accordance with this new existential context to safeguard their respective 'values' or 'essences'.

Lecture Ten
Salvation

In this final lecture, we will elaborate on the nature of salvation as per the Quran and the narrations of the blessed Prophet. Salvation is the subjective or individual component of 'the *dīn* of Allah', and it is the anticipated end (or goal) of human existence on this earth. The principal aim of sending successive prophets and revelations has been to assist the Children of Adam in the purpose of their worldly lives, which is the attainment of salvation: "… but surely there will come to you a guidance from Me, then whoever follows My guidance, no fear shall come upon them, nor shall they grieve." (2:38)

As discussed previously, 'the *dīn* of Allah' or *islām* has been refashioned in and for different contexts with the sole intent of orienting humankind towards God and facilitating their growth to a nobler state. It should be noted that the body and mind, which consists of the soul and Spirit, are in a symbiotic relationship: the growth of each one depends on the other. Since the ideal of 'the nobler state' is the end or goal of each human being, it is greatly beneficial if not necessary for human beings to belong to collectivities that have systems of governance that are most conducive to their rational, moral, and spiritual refinement.

Even though the chances for human beings to actualise 'the nobler state' are greatest in collectivities with systems of governance most conducive to their growth, salvation is essentially an individual, personal or a subjective matter. The sons of prophets Adam and Nuh are condemned in the Quran despite being the children of the prophets of God: Qabil, the son of Prophet Adam, was condemned because of his unwholesome inner state, and the son of Prophet Nuh was condemned due to his rejection of the One True God. Similarly, the wives of prophets Lut and Nuh, and the father of Prophet Ibrahim, are also condemned in the Quran. In contrast, the wife of the Pharaoh is celebrated as a believer par excellence in the Quran and hence is spoken of as an inhabitant of heaven. Similarly, the Youths of the Cave are considered as 'the friends of God' because of their inner orientation towards God, despite not being acquainted with any 'formal' monotheistic faith. This demonstrates that the label of faith, or the mere belonging to an organised 'formal' religion, does not guarantee 'salvation' in and of itself.

Salvation must be understood in existential terms, that is, in terms of 'growth' towards God. In other words, we need to make God our objective – for He is the Most Perfect and Beautiful in every conceivable way – and then evolve towards Him in a directed manner by surrendering to Him, which is the state of *islām*. Thus, salvation is the actualisation of the human potential in the direction of godliness. The Quran addresses the entirety of humankind: "Has there come upon man a time when he was not worthy of mention... Indeed, We have showed him the path; either he is grateful or ungrateful." (76:1-3) Here, gratefulness, or 'being grateful', is an existential state, a state of 'growth' towards God. It is to bring the godly light within into fruition. Ungratefulness, or 'not being grateful', is also an existential state, a state of 'growth' away from God. It is to become alienated from God whereby the soul becomes enwrapped by the ego and its arrogance, and hence the soul and Spirit become concealed.

The Quran describes God as 'the Light': "Allah is the Light of the heavens and the earth...." (24:35) It depicts the motion of His devotees towards Him thus: "… He purges them from darkness and brings them into light…" (2:257). The Quran states that the light of good souls emanate before them and from their hands on the Day of Reckoning, and they will pray: "Our Lord, complete our light for us…". (66:8) In contrast, it describes the people who disbelieve and are condemned as being in a regressive state: "… As for those who disbelieve, their patrons are false deities. They bring them out of light into darkness…" (2:257). It portrays their inner state of turmoil thus: "… [the inner state of their soul is] like the [utter] darkness of the turbulent ocean, covered by waves upon waves, above which is a cloud; [layers of utter] darkness one above another; when he holds out his hand, he is almost unable to see it; and to whomsoever Allah does not give light, he has no light." (24:40)

The Quran also employs the words *khusrān* (loss) and *falāḥ* (success) to this effect, that is, to depict the states of existential completion and incompletion, for instance: "… Say, 'Indeed, the *losers* are those who shall have *lost* themselves and their families on the Day of Resurrection…" (39:15) Regarding the deeds of such 'losers', it states: "As for those who disbelieve, their deeds are like a mirage in a desert assumed by the thirsty person to be water, until, when he comes to it, he finds nothing. Instead, he finds Allah there, and He pays him his account in full…" (24:39) The word *falāḥ* (success) means 'to open up', implying the state of having actualised the fullness of the existential potential. In Arabic, *falāḥ* (success) is often employed to depict a seed that has reached the state of being a fruit bearing tree. Accordingly, the word for 'farmer' in Arabic is *'fallāḥ'*, the one who tills the land, sows seeds, and irrigates and cultivates the land to grow and harvest crops and fruit. Thus, the Quran describes the believers and doers of good deed as *muflihūn* (those who have succeeded): "… those are the successful ones." (2:3-5)

Therefore, 'salvation' and 'damnation' depend on the inner state of our souls. The forms of reward and punishment that souls will experience in Paradise and Hell respectively correspond to the inner states of souls directly (and obviously, the inner states of souls are brought about by the types of deeds performed and the intentions for their performance). Thus, the Quranic dichotomy of 'the friend of God' and 'the enemy of God' are designations for the inner state of our souls, for they are indicative of a soul's relationship with God at a very personal or subjective level. Since God-orientation is an affair of the personal or subjective component of the soul, the possibility of godliness exists in every human being irrespective of whether they adhere to a religion or not.

In our contemporary era, we are witnessing increasing numbers of people in the West who sincerely believe in an Overwhelming Spiritual Reality, live virtuous lives, believe in life beyond the body, and perform righteous deeds, but they do not subscribe to a particular religion or faith system. Most people reading Mawlana Rumi in the West do not belong to any faith-based system. Throughout the history of Islam, there have always been scholars – usually among the mystics and philosophers – who have maintained that rational, moral, and spiritual truths are *perennial* and universal, and hence they have been expressed repeatedly by prophets, philosophers, and saints in all cultures since time immemorial. At no time has the universality of rationality, morality, and spirituality been more evident than it is today when rational, moral, and spiritual 'growth' is patently observable and verifiable in all manner of individuals irrespective of religion or faith.

Exclusivist thinking, which has become prevalent among the people of faith and religion since the European renaissance and colonialism, is indicative of our inner state of deficiency and lack of self-actualisation in godliness. In the creation of God, which is His manifestation, we find only a few thousand criminals imprisoned in a city with a population of five million residents. Then how can we assume that God's Paradise will be empty, and His

Hell filled to the brim? Does the Quran not state, "None but the most wretched shall burn therein"? (92:15) Are the majority of humankind 'wretched people'? The Muslims and *exclusivist* people of faith and religion may counter thus: 'Then why does the Quran use the word *believers* as opposed to *humankind* when referring to the inhabitants of Paradise?' This is an important question that requires a proper response.

The Quran guarantees 'damnation' only for 'the enemies of God' because of their ungodly outlook and inhumane actions. Hence, the Quran declares the possibility of 'salvation' for all other human beings, that is, for all the members of the People of the Book, including all the followers of the blessed Prophet, and for all individuals who do not belong to the Abrahamic faiths. Recall the criterion for 'salvation' as per the verses of the Quran cited earlier: 'salvation' is assured for all who are God-conscious, perform righteous deeds, and believe in the Hereafter irrespective of which tribe, culture, nation, or religion they belong to. Moreover, the Quran relates that the Pharaoh asked Prophet Musa about the state of humankind prior to his prophethood, for presumably they could not classify as 'believers'. Prophet Musa's response was that the knowledge of them is with Allah; he – that blessed Prophet of God – did not pass any judgement (see 20:51-2).

It is not possible for a soul to be the same as another at the subjective or inner level. This is because existential individuality, uniqueness, and plurality, which are the hallmarks of existence generally, necessitate that every soul be unique. It is for this reason that the Quran expresses the maxim of 'non-coercion', for 'coercion' seeks to impose uniformity at the expense of individuality, uniqueness, and plurality; in other words, 'coercion' is an impediment to 'the existential property of growth or self-liberation'. The whole purpose of human existence would be defeated if people were made to submit to God without their own wholesome and wilful surrender. Hence, self-actualisation, which is 'total submission to God', is dependent upon the wholesome and wilful surrender of the individual. The Quran states that had God desired, all on earth would have believed: "Had your Lord willed, all those on earth would have believed altogether. Will you then compel people to become believers?" (10:99)

Thus, every human soul is vested with the potential to consciously return to God by journeying sincerely and surrendering wholesomely. The path to 'salvation' must be traversed by each soul individually. By adopting an attitude of genuine inquiry with the sincere intent to know God, a soul is on its way to realising the sublime state of *islām*. Such a soul will be honoured by God even if it does not reach its goal in this worldly life. As a collective, the only thing that can be done is to create an environment that is conducive for the journey of each individual soul. Let us explain this more clearly.

As handiworks of God possessing His Spirit, we are naturally predisposed to turn towards His Beautiful Reality despite our propensity to be attached to our animalistic bodily constitutions. The Spirit of God yearns to reunite with its Origin from the moment it was blown into humankind. This is the existential state of every human individual irrespective of its persuasions. Consider the following verses of the Quran: "By the soul and That which balanced it; and He inspired it [with a conscience] of what is evil for it and [what is] good for it; he will indeed be successful who purifies it; and he will indeed fail who corrupts it." (91:7-10) and "Indeed, We have ennobled the Children of Adam...". (17:70) These verses assert that the knowledge of good and evil is available to the Children of Adam at the intuitive or existential level of their being. This is because they have been ennobled by having the Spirit of God blown into them, which is driving them towards godly self-actualisation. Therefore, considering firstly their inherent nobility, secondly their intuitive knowledge of good and evil, and thirdly their being chosen as His representatives (*khulafāʾ*) despite the angels forecasting their failure based on their knowledge of human nature, the Children of Adam are destined to come of age and 'grow' towards god-liness, for otherwise the angels would be proven to have been correct about God's selection of humankind as His representatives, which is theologically problematic!

Thus, the only thing that needs to be done is to create an environment conducive to the 'growth' of the human individual. This is what the blessed Prophet did in seventh century Arabia, and this is what the Mahdi will do when he reappears. The hadith literature states that the Mahdi will fill the earth with equity and justice to the degree that injustice and tyranny dominated the world prior to his reappearance. Upon establishing social justice and eliminating poverty, most societal ills, such as lying, cheating and theft, will disappear for they will have no grounds to breed upon, and the natural flowering of 'human nobility' will result in the cessation of promiscuity and most human indecencies. Thus, human souls will be impelled naturally towards the deeper calling of a more substantive spiritual existence. To reiterate, a befitting societal setup and the creation of an environment conducive to human growth is of paramount importance.

Prior to concluding this lecture, we will briefly discuss human purpose and the notions of morality and 'the virtuous deed' as per the Quran.

The Quran presupposes that its audience is aware of the distinction between the human soul, its earthly body, and their respective purposes. The purposes of bodily existence in and of itself include procreation and the procurement of daily nourishment, shelter, and clothing. A body needs a soul for it to be able to function and live, but a soul also needs a body for it to fulfil its purpose during its allotted time on this earth. The purpose of the human soul is expressed in the following verses of the Quran cited in previous lectures: "Indeed, We offered the Trust to the heavens, the earth, and the mountains, yet they refused to undertake it and were afraid of it; and humankind undertook it..." (33:72), "And when your Lord said to the angels, 'I am going to place a steward upon the earth …" (2:30) and "[It is He] Who created death and life to test you, which of you is the best in deeds (*aḥsan ʿamal*)." (67:2) Therefore, the purpose of every human soul is to discharge this 'Trust' by being the steward (*khalīfa*) of God upon this earth and exerting itself fully. This sense of purpose is confirmed in the following verses also cited previously: "… If Allah willed, He would have made you one people (*umma*), but He wanted to test you in what He has given you. So compete [with each other] in good deeds (*khayrāt*)... (5:48) and "And for every [group], there is a direction to which they face. So compete [with each other] in good deeds (*khayrāt*)..." (2:148) The exhortation to perform 'good deeds' and 'the best deeds' is addressed to all of humankind irrespective of their different 'aptitudes', groupings, persuasions, and religions.

These purposes are hardwired into the very being of humankind; in other words, they are existential. Consider our rational and moral evolution: Today we not only explore space, but we affirm the inalienable human rights of every human being, and beyond that we are beginning to recognise the rights of animals and plants. Alongside this rational and moral refinement, there is potential for greater numbers of people to 'awaken' spiritually. To reiterate, the Spirit of God within humankind compels it to 'grow' towards the truth (knowledge of things), the good (moral knowledge), and God (spiritual knowledge). Hence, all of humankind is on the track of self-realisation.

After God announced His intention to place a *khalīfa* (steward) upon the earth, the angels replied: "Will you place therein one who shall cause corruption in it and spill blood?" (2:30) Since our constitution is a composite of the bodily and Spirit (or the worldly and godly), this 'corruption' and 'spilling of blood' is the result of the soul's tendency to favour the bodily/worldly over the Spirit/godly combined with our immense knowledge potential. In fact, there is a constant struggle and tension within each soul as to which side of its bodily-Spirit constitution it will favour in any given moment. Similarly, there is a constant struggle and tension within every smaller and greater collectivity as to which side of the bodily-Spirit constitution they will choose to prioritise. This tension and struggle results in the dynamism necessary for the 'growth' and self-realisation of both the individual and collectivity.

Therefore, in view of this bodily-Spirit constitution and the tension in our souls to choose between them, a befitting environment conducive for human growth is of paramount importance to facilitate the success of both the individual and collectivity. It follows then that the collectivity must ensure that the 'forms' of its societal regulations are moral and universally acceptable to humankind at large so that none of its individuals are impeded in the evolution or growth of their diverse capacities. To ensure that the 'forms' of its societal regulations are moral and universal, they must be fashioned on the basis of 'the existential property of growth' and 'the principle of justice' as appreciated by the degree of growth of 'human nobility' in any given time and place.

The Quran exhorts that all human norms, such as human interactions with one another, the environment, animals, and plants, must be based on 'the principle of justice' and 'human nobility'. Such societal regulations apply to humankind *as humankind*, that is, to all individuals irrespective of faith or religion. Consider the following verses revealed during the Meccan period that appealed to the faculties of intuition and reason directly and hence had a positive impact upon the Meccans and visiting Medinan pilgrims: "Indeed, Allah commands justice and generosity, and giving to kinsfolk; and He forbids indecency and the reprehensible and oppression…". (16:90) and

> *Say [O Prophet], 'Come! I will recite what your Lord has forbidden to you: Do not associate anything with Him and show kindness to your parents; do not kill your children on account of [the fear of] poverty; We provide for you and for them; do not come near indecencies, whether open or concealed; and do*

not take a human life, made sacred by Allah, except by [legal]
right. Thus does He command you that you may understand.
And do not come near the wealth of the orphan, unless intending
to enhance it, until they reach maturity, and give full measure
and weight with justice; We task not any soul save to its capac-
ity; and when you speak, be just, even though it be [against]
a close relative; and fulfil your covenant with Allah. Thus
does He command you that you may be mindful. (6:151–2)

Upon hearing these verses, the Medinan pilgrims understood that the Prophet was referring to societal ills that had been plaguing their societies. They conveyed these teachings to the people of Medina upon their return. Subsequently, they invited the Prophet to preside over them despite the majority of Medina not having embraced Islam at the time. This demonstrates that what they heard from the Prophet was rational and moral, and hence intuitively understandable by humans *as humans*. Thus, 'the *dīn* of Allah', and its most recent expression – 'Islam', have always been in sync with human nature.

Therefore, at the level of the global human collectivity, there is a need to articulate and form an all-embracing moral culture whose values, norms, rights, and duties are common to and upheld by one and all, thereby uniting all people as one humankind. Obviously, such a system or culture would be based on 'the principle of justice', 'human nobility' and 'the existential property of growth', for a moral system is one that is just, noble, and growth-promoting by definition. Its values, norms, rights, and duties would accrue or be modified as and when 'human nobility' grows and evolves.

Giving life, caring for others, kindness, fair play, and human decency are examples of norms and values that emanate naturally from 'human nobility' (the innate sense of compassion, decency, and godliness in humankind). They manifest with greater intensity as humankind 'grows', and then they in turn inform the derivation of regulations and rights at every level of the collectivity accordingly. Such norms and values are understood by our faculty of intuition as true and good because they are existentially productive. The faculty of intuition can know instantaneously that which is existentially productive because its ground (or source) is 'existence' *as Spirit* (or 'human nobility'), the nature of which is to be productive, growth-promoting, and self-realising. As individuals gain an ever-refined sense of 'human nobility', it causes their faculties of intuition to prompt them directly or through rational arguments to greater levels of human actualisation as explained in the previous lecture.

Ironically, those labelled by us as 'irreligious' uphold 'the principle of justice' the most and are the most charitable and compassionate towards God's creatures. For instance, those who fight for justice and the rights of the 'other', regardless of the 'other's' persuasion, culture, gender, sex, religion, faith, and/or country of residence, are people of 'no-faith' (in Europe and North America) predominantly. Again, discussions on animal welfare, environmental crises, and slave labour have not been given their due attention by religious organisations generally. Similarly, charity given by theocratic states to the needy of the world is insignificant when compared to the charity given by the so-called 'irreligious' residents of secular states. Finally, the welfare, education, and medical systems in secular states are incomparably better than those in Muslim states. These things need to be thought through carefully.

Human progression culminates in that deep sense of spiritual purpose and 'growth' towards God Who is the Peak of human aspirations. The only reason people turn away from God is because organised faiths and religions have misrepresented Him. Otherwise, how is it possible for any heart to resist the deep calling within? The Quran states: "And who would turn away from the *milla* of Ibrahim except one who has fooled himself..." (2:130). The good people of our world are not foolish at heart; on the contrary, they are good people, and in fact they are doing God's work better than the faithful of all religions. They are searching for the deeper meaning, but the organised faiths and religions have failed to portray the Beauty, Goodness, and Truth of God in their interpretations of God's communications. In any case, the fundamental requirement of 'the *dīn* of Allah' with respect to the global human collectivity is the creation of institutions and the formulation of regulations on the basis of 'the existential property of growth', 'the principle of justice', and 'human nobility'.

The second topic of our brief survey is 'spiritual morality' and 'the attainment of the virtuous state'. 'Spiritual morality' refers to the God-oriented attitude of the inner or subjective aspect of the soul during its execution of both devotional and societal regulations. The phrase 'the attainment of the virtuous state' signifies the realisation of the connection between the heart of the soul and God. It is the fruit of constantly practicing 'spiritual morality'. In other words, it is the effect of the soul performing all devotional acts and fulfilling all societal regulations with the intention of gaining proximity to Allah. It should be noted that 'the attainment of the virtuous state' is not restricted to Muslims. In fact, it is the natural state of all *muslim*s, that is, of all souls surrendered to God totally. Thus, one finds souls who have 'attained the virtuous state' in every Abrahamic faith and every religious/spiritual system that believes in the One Supremely Perfect God, just like in the examples of the Quran which we have cited previously.

The ideal of 'God-orientation of the subjective/inner aspect of the soul' is supposed to be a perpetual state; hence, it is not to be sought during the performance of devotional acts only, rather we are also supposed to seek it during the implementation of all 'non-religious' societal, secular, and/or purely rational norms, duties, regulations, and interactions. In this respect, the Quran employs certain terms which we need to discuss briefly.

The Quran employs the phrase 'righteous deed' ('*amal ṣāliḥ* in Arabic) in the verses that promise salvation to all the sincere and genuine adherents of the Abrahamic faiths:

Indeed, those who believe (that is, the followers of Prophet Mu-hammad), and the Jews, Christians, and Sabians, whoever [amongst them] has faith in Allah and the Last Day and does righteous deeds, they will have their reward with their Lord, and there is no fear for them, nor shall they grieve. (2:62)

Indeed, those who believe (that is, the followers of the Prophet Muhammad), and the Jews, Sabians, and Christians, whoever [amongst them] has faith in Allah and the Last Day and does good deeds, they shall have no fear, nor shall they grieve. (5:69)

There is a general agreement among scholars that the phrase *'amal ṣāliḥ* in the Quran refers to the prescribed 'forms' of the devotional regulations; in other words, it refers to those acts which when performed engender the attitude of God-centricity and the sense of 'religious' identity in the minds of its practitioners. Obviously, these are *ṣalāt, ṣawm, ḥajj* and *zakāt*. Now since these verses are using the phrase *'amal ṣāliḥ* with respect to the sincere and genuine adherents of the Abrahamic faiths, it is being used in these verses to refer to the performance of the 'forms' of devotional regulations of each of the Abrahamic faiths and not just the Muslim 'forms'. However, the mere performance of the 'forms' of devotional regulations (irrespective of whether they are the 'forms' of Muslims or the other Abrahamic faiths) does not constitute *'amal ṣāliḥ*; rather, only the performance of the 'form' that is accompanied with the attitude of God-centricity qualifies as *'amal ṣāliḥ*. This is because both verses connect the *'amal ṣāliḥ* of the Jews, Christians, and Sabians with the belief in God and Hereafter. In other words, both verses are referring to those Jews, Christians, and Sabians who are sincere, genuine, and deeply conscious of God and of meeting with Him, and hence they are focused on God during their respective devotional practices.

To reiterate, the verses of the Quran acknowledge that God has prescribed different devotional practices to each of the Abrahamic faiths, and that they all have the potential to qualify as 'amal ṣāliḥ. This means that the physical or outward 'forms' of the devotional regulations of the Muslims are not 'amal ṣāliḥ in and of themselves, rather they are means to 'amal ṣāliḥ. This is because the Quran classifies the God-conscious performance of the 'forms' of the Jewish and Christian devotional regulations as 'amal ṣāliḥ as well, which it would not do if only the performance of the 'forms' of the Muslim devotional regulations classified as 'amal ṣāliḥ exclusively.

The salvific aspect of 'amal ṣāliḥ lies in the effect of its performance, which is the refinement and enlightenment of the soul, and not in its mere ritualistic and habitual performance. This is made clear by the statements of the blessed Prophet and Imam Ali, such as: 'Ṣalāt is accepted if it brings about a positive change within the soul.' The acceptance of the performance of a devotional regulation is dependent upon whether the performance has resulted in the inner growth of the soul (or in other words, in a meaningful connection with God). The procurement of Paradise in the Hereafter is to be viewed as a consequence of the soul's dedicated devotion, worship, and service to God. Thus, it is possible for every adherent of the Abrahamic faiths to perform their respective devotional regulations with the attitude of God-centricity, whereby their performance would classify as 'amal ṣāliḥ.

The Quran also employs the term *khayrāt* (good deeds) to refer to God-centred actions. *Khayrāt* are commonly understood to be altruistic actions, that is, actions performed for the good of others. The Quranic usage is slightly different; it terms altruistic actions performed with the attitude of God-centricity as *khayrāt*. Thus, *khayrāt* comprise all those familial, communal, societal, and environmental interactions of the believer that are accompanied with the believer's intention of gaining the good pleasure of God. The Quran uses the term in the context of the blessed prophets: "And We made them leaders who guided [people] by Our command, and We inspired in them the doing of good deeds (*khayrāt*)..." (21:73). It also employs the term with respect to the actions of Prophet Zakariya, his wife, and his son, Prophet Yahya: "Verily, they would hasten to do good deeds (*khayrāt*)." (21:90)

Therefore, *khayrāt* are deeds that are beneficial to humankind, such as charity, forgiveness, social service, reconciliation, education, and discovery, performed with the attitude of God-centricity. As with *al-ʿamal al-ṣāliḥ* (the righteous deed), it is possible for the adherents of the Abrahamic faiths and other monotheistic religions to perform actions that qualify as *khayrāt* in the Quranic sense. The following verses of the Quran exhort the adherents of the Abrahamic faiths to compete in *khayrāt*: "And for every [group], there is a direction to which they face. So compete [with each other] in good deeds (*khayrāt*)..." (2:148) and "... If Allah willed, He would have made you one people (*umma*), but He wanted to test you in what He has given you. So compete [with each other] in good deeds (*khayrāt*)... (5:48) Hence, the possibility of the performance of *khayrāt* is not restricted to the Muslim. In fact, only the actions of the *muslim* (that is, one totally surrendered to God beyond theological beliefs) truly qualify as *khayrāt* in the Quranic sense.

In contrast, deeds performed by 'the enemies of God' that seem to be 'good' and beneficial for humankind do not qualify as *khayrāt*. This is because selfless love for all of humankind is part and parcel of godliness. An 'enemy of God' by definition stands in opposition to godly values, and hence is incapable of selfless love for all of humankind. As for those godly souls who genuinely love all of humankind and consequently contribute to humanity but are either unaware or genuinely unconvinced about the existence of God, they do not classify as 'the enemies of God'. In their case, God's Mercy and Justice gives us surety that they will not be dealt with unjustly by Him in the Hereafter. (For instance, see 17:71, 18:49, and 21:47)

The Quran also employs the terms *ḥasanāt* and *sayyiʾāt* to refer to good and evil deeds respectively. For instance: "Whoever brings a good deed (*ḥasana*), he shall have ten like it, and whoever brings an evil deed (*sayyiʾa*), he shall be recompensed only with the like of it, and they shall not be dealt with unjustly." (6:160) Deliberation upon such verses reveals that the Quran's employment of the words *ḥasana* and *sayyiʾa*, in this sense of remuneration in the Hereafter, is based on the existential properties of our worldly existence. The world responds to the goodness of human beings asymmetrically, that is, it yields significantly more goodness in response to the good deeds of humans especially when they are performed with sincere intentions. In contrast, the world responds to the evil deeds of humans in kind, that is, its response is proportional to their actions, after which it reverts to its natural state of equilibrium and productivity. Thus, the Quran implies that the performance of *ḥasanāt* (good deeds) and *sayyiʾāt* (evil deeds) have consequences in the Hereafter similar quantitatively to the reactions they elicit in this world. This presupposes that its primary audience would have been aware that their good and bad deeds have asymmetrical and symmetrical reactions in this world respectively. Hence, the believer should know that the *ḥasanāt* performed in this world will yield significantly more fruits in the Hereafter, whereas *sayyiʾāt* will yield an equal but detrimental reaction.

The Quran employs two terms closely associated with *ḥasana*: *aḥsan* and *muḥsin*. They are translated as 'the best deed' and 'one who is generous' respectively. Their literal translations are 'the most beautiful' and 'the beautifier'. The Prophet defined 'beautification' (*iḥsān*) as 'the performance of deeds with the awareness that Allah is watching over you.' Thus, *iḥsān* is the beautification of a deed by performing it with the awareness of God's Presence and with the intention of seeking His Proximity. This seems to be what is referred to whenever the Quran employs the phrase "*aḥsanu ʿamalan*" (best in deeds): "… We will most certainly give them their reward for the best of what they did." (16:97)

Iḥsān is also used in the sense of 'doing more than what a recipient deserves with the intention of seeking proximity to Allah and His pleasure'. For instance, the Quran states: "…Respond with what is *aḥsan* (better), then see the enmity between you and him change as though he was your close friend" (41:34), "…Do better (*aḥsin*), as Allah has done better for you (*aḥsan*)…" (28:77), and "[It is He] Who created death and life to test you, which of you is the best in deeds (*aḥsan ʿamal*); and He is the Mighty, the Forgiving." (67:2) Thus, *iḥsān* is to do 'more good' to one's family, community, society, and environment with the attitude of God-centricity. The Quran states that 'salvation' is guaranteed for those who have surrendered to God and perform beautiful works: "Nay, but whoever surrenders his whole self to Allah, and he is doer of beautiful works (*muḥsin*), he has his reward with his Lord, and they will have no fear, nor shall they grieve." (2:112). Therefore, the culmination of God-orientation is when the awareness of God accompanies every deed. Thereafter, the performance of every deed is naturally beautiful and perfect, for every deed issues from and is accompanied by the God-conscious activity of the heart. Again, such verses are generic and hence apply to all who have surrendered to Allah and are *muḥsinīn* (doers of beautiful works) irrespective of their faith or religion.

Therefore, the various 'forms' of 'the *dīn* of Allah' seek to engender a God-centric orientation in their respective adherents by exhorting them to practice *iḥsān* in all areas of human life, be they devotional or societal. Hence, they encourage their respective adherents to cultivate the awareness of the Presence of God during even the most mundane aspects of human life, such as the buying and selling of goods. In other words, the awareness of the Omnipresence of Allah is not restricted to the devotional regulations ordained by religion, rather it must accompany the believer during all their non-devotional societal interactions too. The Quran exhorts humankind to be just during business transactions and to ensure that due measures are given as per the contract. The

Prophet taught that *iḥsān* in the domain of business transactions means to take less payment than the price set, and to give more of the goods than what is due, with the intention of seeking proximity to Allah and His pleasure.

To summarise, for actions to classify as *ʿamal ṣāliḥ, khayrāt, ḥasanāt,* or *iḥsān,* they must be accompanied by the soul's awareness of God. Such actions are existential because they refine us rationally, morally, and spiritually, and hence they are means to salvation and Paradise. They can be performed by any human being irrespective of faith or religion. One does not have be a Muslim to perform such actions. In fact, such actions issue forth from those who have totally submitted to God beyond the theological beliefs of any religion or faith (*muslims*) naturally, spontaneously, and perpetually; theirs is the religion of *islām* — the Religion *beyond* religion. Finally, it is possible for all human beings to perform *khayrāt* (good deeds) irrespective of whether they believe in God or not so long as they are sincere, genuine, good, and decent. However, it is impossible for those belonging to the category of 'enemy of God' to perform actions qualifying as '*khayrāt*', irrespective of whether they are Muslims, Christians, Jews, Hindus, Buddhists, atheists, or agnostics.

Final Word

Such is the broad vision of the Islam of the Quran and the blessed Prophet – the final expression of the *perennial* and fluid *'dīn* of Allah'. The ideal human society, according to the Islam of the Quran and the blessed Prophet, is the moral society, for it is conducive to the rational, moral, and spiritual growth of one and all without coercion. The spiritual identities of the different Abrahamic faiths are to be honoured for they are all equal spiritually. Salvation is only dependent upon the degree of God-centricity of the subjective or inner aspect of the soul; hence, it is a possibility for one and all irrespective of religion, faith, or any other persuasion. Epistemic inaccuracies of the other religious traditions were never viewed as being fundamentally problematic in the Islam of the Quran and the blessed Prophet. The faithful were advised to engage in dialogue and share knowledge in a most befitting manner. The purpose of this dialogue was to form a greater collectivity among the People of the Book and the other monotheistic religions on the basis of their shared belief in and worship of the One True God.

Finally, the following is a tribute to our beloved Imam Husayn. It is a paraphrased rendering of sections of the supplication he recited a year prior to his martyrdom at the foot of Mount Raḥma on the plains of ʿArafāt:

O Lord, when were You hidden that I needed to see You?
Blind are the eyes that do not see You watch over them. O

Lord, when were You at a distance that I needed to come close to You? You have always been close; it is I who has remained at a distance from You. O Lord, Your Mercy does not require a cause for It to embrace me, how then should my good works be a cause for Your Mercy to descend upon me? O Lord, Your Beauty knows no bounds; as soon as we get accustomed to one level of Your Being, You show us another glimpse leaving our hearts yearning for more. O Lord, how unworthy I am! O Lord, how wonderful You are! O Lord, I am a poor man despite being wealthy. O Lord, allow me not to yearn for something that You have destined to keep away from me. O Lord, allow me not to yearn the hastening of a decree that You have delayed. O Lord, allow me not to yearn the delay of a decree that You have hastened.